Forbidden Glory

Portraits of Pride

Forbidden
Glory

Portraits of Pride

---

by

Judson Cornwall

McDougal Publishing is a ministry of The McDougal Foundation, Inc., a Maryland nonprofit corporation dedicated to spreading the Gospel of the Lord Jesus Christ to as many people as possible in the shortest time possible.

Published by:

McDougal Publishing
P.O. Box 3595
Hagerstown, MD 21742-3595
www.mcdougalpublishing.com

ISBN 1-58158-051-7

Printed in the United States of America
For Worldwide Distribution

DEDICATION

I dedicate this book to Nancy Lambert—a personal friend and gifted motivator. Without her pleading, urging, and encouragement, this book would not have been written.

ACKNOWLEDGMENTS

My thanks go to the following people for reading the manuscript. Your input and comments were valuable and appreciated:

Sue Curran	Stelman Smith
Joe Johnson	Ann Stevenson
Nancy Lambert	Terri Terry
Christian Senftleben	Iverna Tompkins
Norbert Senftleben	Steve Vanzant

Ressa and Deidre Slaybaugh

My heartfelt thanks to my good friend, Dr. Joe Johnson, pastor of Grace Lutheran Church in Show Low, Arizona, for preparing the questions that follow each chapter. They not only stimulate review, but they induce further thought on the subject matter.

CONTENTS

PREFACE

All twelve hundred seats were filled with worshipers, the overflow seating was full, and people were standing in the hallway at the Exaltation Conference in Columbus, Ohio. The keynote speaker, Rev. Stephen Fry, introduced his theme by recounting the many different prayer programs that are being used in America today. He said, "There probably has never been a time in our history when so much prayer has been offered to God in the United States of America. Why does it seem to be so ineffective? Because of our pride, for *pride neutralizes prayer.*"

He had my immediate attention, for I had just completed the manuscript for this book. Still, I had not thought of pride as being a great neutralizer to prayer. As I thought about it, I realized that he was right. God pays very little attention to the prayer of the proud. He is looking for a humble heart and a contrite spirit. It is almost certain that we would all profit from a greater emphasis on humility before God. Then our prayer will again become effective and powerful.

While writing this book, I wrestled with myself as I saw how much my own life had been dominated by pride. In the process I found answers to questions I really did not want to ask. Tears of repentance and regret have flowed down my cheeks as I typed the truths that now make up the contents of this book. How I hope each chapter will bring the readers to some of the places of repentance that I have experienced. If it doesn't, it has been worth writing the book...just to learn more about myself.

There would be no need for a study on pride if it were merely an unpleasant personality trait. Unfortunately, this is not the case. Out-of-control pride is an extremely destructive force—both to the proud person and to those around him or her.

There are those among us who say that pride is a demonic activity.

I could almost wish that they were right, for Christ has given the believer complete authority over the demonic realm. We could simply cast out "the demon of pride" and see a person permanently delivered from it. We all know that this just doesn't work in practical experience, for while our enemy will cultivate the pride within us, he is not its originator—he cannot plant it.

Jesus taught us that pride is not a force without us—it is a power within us, and no one is exempt from its presence in his or her life. Somehow it seems that the more we wrestle with it, the stronger it becomes. Self-treatment will not cure us of our pride. God's prescription is to replace pride with humility, and this often requires radical transplant surgery.

Surgery, however, is preceded by examination: x-rays, CAT scans, and lab tests. That's the ministry of this book. The transplant will come in Chapter 21.

Judson Cornwall
Phoenix, Arizona

Part I

THE SCOPE OF THE PROBLEM

Chapter 1

PRIDE: OUR GREATEST ENEMY

I prefer to read the writings of the experienced, not just those written by theorists. Before I read a book on cooking, I would like to know that the author was a chef, or at least a person very competent in the kitchen. If the author hasn't experienced cooking, how could he or she teach me anything about it?

One of the first things I did after entering Southern California Bible College, back in the early forties, was to form a trumpet trio. One of the students, whom I'll call Henry, approached us and offered to give us trumpet lessons at the discount rate of three for the price of one. It sounded great to us and we signed up for a series of lessons. Imagine our disappointment when, on our first lesson, we learned that Henry could not play the trumpet. He was a guitarist. Somehow we did not feel that his experience in strings would translate well to brass, so we canceled the lessons.

I want you to know that I have experienced pride. Boy, have I experienced it! I have more than observed and read about it. I have been there. I write from the pain that pride has produced in me and, worse than that, from the memory of how my pride has hurt others.

I do not write this book as an expert in humility. I write it as one who has played my pride instrument for many years. I think I can recognize the tones of pride in almost any key and any tempo. I don't suppose that this will be a very popular book, and perhaps only the brave will read it. I agree with my publisher, however, that it is an important book for all Christians today.

One day, just after I began writing the book, I was checking in for a Northwest Airlines flight from Phoenix to Minneapolis. Before handing me my ticket envelope, the agent deftly grabbed the handles of the smaller bag I had checked in, intending to lightly flip it onto the moving conveyor belt. She succeeded only in dragging it onto the floor. Shocked, she said, "This must be full of tools."

"Not tools," I said, "books! One of the disadvantages of being a writer is that people expect me to bring some of my books to my speaking engagements."

This time using both hands, she successfully placed the bag on the belt. "You're an author?" she asked. "What are you writing now?"

This wasn't the standard question I am asked when my identity as an author is discovered. Most people want to know what I have written. She put it in the present tense—wanting to know what I was currently working on.

Regaining my composure, I said, "I'm writing a book tentatively titled *Portraits of Pride*."

"A book on pride?" she asked. "No one will buy it. This is the most self-centered generation in history."

With that, she handed me my ticket and prepared to check in the next traveler. I appreciated her observation and thanked her, but it didn't sway me from finishing the book. After all, our Lord has taught us:

> *The fear of the* Lord *is to hate evil: pride, and arrogancy, and the evil way, and the froward mouth, do I hate.*
>
> Proverbs 8:13

Perhaps my writing this book is like the pastor preaching to the choir. I do not apologize for that, for the choir of believers and their respective leaders desperately need to take another look at the original sin produced by pride. Pride induced the downfall of the mighty angel Lucifer, and it has been responsible for the downfall of many powerful ministers since then. Pride will pull us away from God, too, unless we learn His answer to it.

We cannot expect nonbelievers in Christ to be concerned with pride, for that is one leg of the three-legged stool upon which their lives rest. Both God's Kingdom and the world's system are built on a triad of principles. Paul tells us, *"For the kingdom of God is...righteousness, and peace, and joy in the Holy Ghost"* (Romans 14:17), while the apostle John wrote, *"All that is in the world, the lust of the flesh, and the lust of the eyes, and the pride of life, is not of the Father, but is of the world"* (1 John 2:16). We have to determine which three-legged stool we will rest our lives upon. We can't sit on both of them simultaneously. Our life's foundation will either be *"righteousness, peace, and joy in the Holy Ghost,"* or it will be *"the lust of the flesh, and the lust of the eyes, and the pride of life."*

Pride may well be a permanent fixture in the world, but Jesus told us, *"Ye are not of the world, but I have chosen you out of the world"* (John 15:19). We are citizens of Heaven who have been positioned on earth as heavenly ambassadors (see 2 Corinthians 5:20). We are here, not to be like the world, but to show the world what the heavenly kingdom is like. If we do not reflect the character of God's Kingdom, we are unworthy ambassadors who deserve to be recalled.

Although almost all Christians understand this, we still have an innate pride level with which to contend. I dare not declare that all pride is sin, for that would be going beyond what the Bible tells us, but we must admit that pride is inherent to our sinful nature. We were born with pride. Perhaps the challenge that lies before us is to control that pride rather than allow that pride to control us.

Of all the things my mother said to me during my maturing years, nothing was more meaningful to me than her words, "Son, I'm proud of you." Accordingly, I passed this word of praise to my children, and I often find it lifts a Christian leader's countenance to tell him or her, "I'm proud of you." I think we know what we mean when we make such statements, but we are actually using the wrong word. We mean to say that we are pleased with them or with their actions. We are trying to convey to them our sense of satisfaction.

Pride Is Negative

We have to read deep in the dictionary definition of *pride* or *proud* to find a hint of justification for using this word positively. Pride is consistently defined in negative terms. Its synonyms speak of arrogance, insolence, and disdainfulness. Pride is always condemned throughout the Bible. It is never viewed as a positive attitude. Take a few moments with a Bible concordance and search Bible verses with the word "pride" in them. You won't find a single verse that speaks of pride in a positive manner. God sees pride as a serious negative in anyone's life. And it is dangerous for us to view pride differently than God views it.

If pride is basically a "bad" thing, why is there so much of it in our lives? Where do we learn to be proud? Who is the teacher of pride? Or is it even a learned behavior? Do we ingest it by observing others, or do we inherit it from our parents? Maybe it comes from a source outside ourselves.

Our nation is dangerously obsessed with pride. We could wonder if any nation has ever been more preoccupied with pride than is the United States of America. Our young men are challenged to be among "the few, the proud, the Marines." Advertisers tell us we will be ultimately proud to have their car seen in our driveway. Patriotism calls for us to sing, "I'm so proud to be called an American," while every parent is proud of his or her offspring. We glamorize pride in our persons, possessions, positions, and prestige. It was reported that in 1999 almost twice as many people underwent laser cosmetic procedures to recapture their youth than in 1988.[1] We are, indeed, a proud people. Is this good or bad for our nation?

Even more pertinent is the question" Why is the Church in America so proud? Mike Yaconelli, in his book *The Door*, said, "Let's—all of us—decide to stop trying to convince the world that Christianity is true because Jesus makes us prettier, happier, thinner, wealthier, bigger, more successful, more popular, healthier, stronger, and more influential than everyone else. Do we actually believe that the world is impressed with our fancy new churches, 12,000 in Sunday school, five services each morning, the 'millions' who are watching on television, converted beauty queens and professional athletes, our book sales, or our crusades? The world is laughing at us—mocking us and the Jesus we supposedly are serving."[2]

Those are strong words that go against the grain of popular religious thought in America, but they are good, challenging words. Pride among us is destroying more than the Holy Spirit is producing within us. Certainly this cannot be classified as "good." As we have said, this is the cause of the fall of many highly visible ministers and ministries.

Pride Unmasked

God explicitly declares that He hates pride (see Proverbs 8:13), and He further warns us, *"Pride goes before destruction, a haughty spirit before a fall"* (Proverbs 16:18, NIV). Both statements seem to go against our modern concept of pride, but are we just trying to make something good out of something bad?

The word *pride* is not a recent addition to our English vocabulary. It is a very old word that describes an attitude that is older than mankind itself. It did not have its beginnings on earth, but in Heaven.

Richard Newton, who lived in the mid-1800s, said, "Let me give you the history of pride in three small chapters. The beginning of pride was in heaven. The continuance of pride is on earth. The end of pride is in hell. This history shows how unprofitable it is."[3]

Funk & Wagnall's New Practical Standard Dictionary gives almost three inches of space to its definition of the word *pride*, while the *Merriam-Webster's Seventh New Collegiate Dictionary* condenses its definition to: "(1) the quality or state of being proud—inordinate self-esteem—conceit; (2) a reasonable or justifiable self-respect—delight or elation arising from some act or possession; (3) proud or disdainful behavior or treatment—disdain; (4) ostentatious display; (5) something that excites pride."[4]

These definitions of pride are not very complimentary, are they? The picture is even bleaker if we look at synonyms and analogous words that are given as substitute words for *pride. Webster's New Dictionary of Synonyms* gives a full ten inches of space to these substitute words for pride. *The Synonym Finder,* by J.I. Rodale, lists fifteen synonyms for pride that begin with the word *self*: "self-esteem, self-importance, self-exaltation, self-glorification, self-satisfaction, self-content, self-praise, self-laudation, self-gratulation, self-love, self-endearment, self-worship, self-approval, self-approbation, and self-applause." No wonder, then, that the word *pride* is spelled with a big "I" in the middle—*p-r-I-d-e.*

Pride's Universality

The heart of pride is exposed in this acrostic:

> P lease
> R ealize
> I
> D eserve
> E xaltation.

The very fact that "I" is the center and the heart of *pride*, just as it is the center of *sIn,* makes it universal. If there is a person, there is pride. It doesn't matter what the station of that person in life may be. I have seen uneducated, depressed people living in abject poverty who were very proud. I've visited people living in crude huts in the jungles of Africa who were extremely proud of something. Conversely, of course, I've had occasion to fellowship with wealthy people in Europe and America who, too, were very proud. There seems to be no standard of living or amount of possessions that does not trigger pride. The pride is in the individual, and he or she will find an object upon which to project that pride. By focusing their pride on something outside of themselves, people hope to escape responsibility for being proud of themselves.

Pride's Uniqueness

The destructive work of pride goes almost unchecked, primarily because we do not see it at work. Pride wears many masks and offers a great variety of sensations. As someone has said, "Pride is the only disease that everyone suffers from except yourself."[5] It is unlikely that we will see pride in ourselves. I certainly failed to see it in myself...until God began to deal extensively with me on this subject.

By way of this book, let's take a walk through the Bible and see the pride evident in the lives of twenty or more Bible characters, in both the Old and the New Testament. Most of the time the word *pride* will not be found in the Bible story text, but the power and progression of pride proves to be the heart of the problem.

Each of these Bible illustrations of pride wears a different disguise and seems very unlike the preceding story, but that is the ultimate danger of pride: it is multifaceted. It can change its appearance faster than a chameleon can. By the time we feel we understand it in one of its manifestations, pride changes its costume, alters its voice, and deceives us again. Paul said, *"For sin...deceived me"* (Romans 7:11). Unquestionably, pride is the most deceptive of sins.

Now, watch with me a parade of pride...from Heaven to earth...in individuals and in nations. See it at work in families, in prophets, in God appointed leaders, and in churches. Cringe with me as we watch men who are called by God act so pridefully that they become misleaders. Let the Holy Spirit update these stories and make them real to your heart today. Human nature has not changed, and neither have the tactics of our enemy. If we can learn from the examples of others, we can be spared the destruction that happened to them...through pride.

Endnotes:

1. *Popular Science Magazine*, February 2001.
2. Mike Yaconelli, As quoted in *Christianity Today*, Vol. 34, No. 2 (Sept./Oct. 1989).
3. James S. Hewett, *Illustrations Unlimited* (Wheaton, Il.: Tyndale House Publishers, Inc., 1988).
4. *Merriam Webster's Seventh New Collegiate Dictionary* (Chicago: G.& C. Merriam Co., 1972).
5. James S. Hewett, *Illustrations Unlimited* (Wheaton, Il.: Tyndale House Publishers, Inc., 1988).

Dear Heavenly Father,

I am so full of pride it scares me! I'm not sure I even want to read any further in this book, for it will expose more levels of my pride in action. Please give me the grace to read on and to deal honestly with every level of pride I see in myself. I want to be humble in Your sight (at least my spirit does), but my mind and will hold tenaciously to their sense of self-worth. I don't want You to have to humiliate me to crush my pride, so I ask for the work of Your Spirit to enable me to deal with my pride step-by-step. Thank You for the revelation of my inner nature and for the grace to deal with it.

In Jesus' name,
Amen!

• • •

Questions

1. What do you hope to accomplish by reading this book on pride? As you read, ask the Holy Spirit to show you pride in your own life.

2. In what areas do you already recognize pride in your life?

3. What is deceptive about pride?

4. How would you define pride in your own words?

5. Whom do you see as a prideful person? Whom do you see as a humble person? What is different about these two people?

Chapter 2

THE ORIGINS OF PRIDE

How art thou fallen from heaven, O Lucifer, son of the morning! how art thou cut down to the ground, which didst weaken the nations! For thou hast said in thine heart, I will ascend into heaven, I will exalt my throne above the stars of God: I will sit also upon the mount of the congregation, in the sides of the north: I will ascend above the heights of the clouds; I will be like the most High. Isaiah 14:12-14

Son of man, take up a lamentation upon the king of Tyrus, and say unto him, Thus saith the Lord GOD; Thou sealest up the sum, full of wisdom, and perfect in beauty. Thou hast been in Eden the garden of God; every precious stone was thy covering, the sardius, topaz, and the diamond, the beryl, the onyx, and the jasper, the sapphire, the emerald, and the carbuncle, and gold: the workmanship of thy tabrets and of thy pipes was prepared in thee in the day that thou wast created. Thou art the anointed cherub that covereth; and I have set thee so: thou wast upon the holy mountain of God; thou hast walked up and down in the midst of the stones of fire. Thou wast perfect in thy ways from the day that thou wast created, till iniquity was found in thee. By the multitude of thy merchandise they have filled the midst of thee with violence, and thou hast sinned: therefore I will cast thee as profane out of the mountain of God: and I will destroy thee, O covering cherub, from the midst of the stones of fire. Thine heart was lifted up because of thy beauty, thou hast corrupted thy wisdom by reason of thy brightness: I will cast thee to the ground, I will lay thee before kings, that they may behold thee. Thou hast defiled thy sanctuaries by the multitude of thine iniquities, by the iniquity of thy traffic; therefore will I bring forth a fire from the midst of thee, it shall devour thee, and I will bring thee to ashes upon the earth in the sight of all them that behold thee. Ezekiel 28:12-18

*I*t is no secret that very large spiritual, or religious, organizations predated the discovery of America. The founder of the largest of these allowed his followers to call him "Governor." As the organization multiplied its adherents, the Governor began training a huge staff to minister to the "believers," or "followers." Eventually this staff became so large that the Governor divided it into three departments and placed three of his best students as supervisors. History suggests that their names were Lucy, Gabbie, and Mike.

They seemed to serve as equals for a long season, but Lucy showed more initiative and skill than Gabbie and Mike did, and he soon found himself with more supervisory responsibility than the others. The Governor took Lucy on as a personal protégé and poured his knowledge, spiritual power, and organizational skills into him. Lucy soon became the Governor's right-hand man. No one in the entire organization had more authority than Lucy...except, of course, the Governor.

Lucy received orders and authority from the Governor and shared these with the ones chosen to perform a mission. When the business was completed, they reported to Lucy, who, in turn, gave the report to the Governor. In a sense, Lucy was the middleman.

Somewhere in the chain of events, Lucy began to believe that he was actually equal to the Governor. Everyone in the organization looked up to him, received their authority from him, and shared their glorious reports with him. This started to go to his head, and Lucy began a slow progression of pride that led him to proclaim himself an equal to the Governor, and finally to say he was superior to the Governor and would replace him.

No one in the organization understood why the Governor delayed action so long. Surely he knew what was happening, didn't he? Did he feel that he could win back the loyalty of Lucy or bring him back to humility?

History does not record if the Governor waited too long to deal with this prideful rebellion in Lucy, but when the Governor dismissed his right-hand man, Lucy took with him somewhere around a third of the staff and began an organization of his own.

Many pastors can relate this simple parable to their own experience, as trusted assistants rise up in pride and take members of the congregation down the street three blocks to start a rival congregation.

But that is not what this parable is all about. Change the name of the Governor to "Father," and call Lucy "Lucifer," Gabbie "Gabriel," and Mike "Michael," and you'll find yourself looking at the story unfolded in Isaiah and Ezekiel. It is the story of Lucifer's progression of pride and his ultimate expulsion from Heaven.

Self-exaltation in Heaven

Although the Isaiah passage is directed to the king of Babylon and the Ezekiel message was spoken against the king of Tyrus, I agree with the many Bible scholars who see both messages as classic examples of prophetic perspective, which simply means that there are at least two interpretations—one near at hand and one far away. There are far too many things said in these passages that cannot refer solely to earthly monarchs for it to be otherwise.

Eugene Peterson uses contemporary idioms to make these passages come alive. He writes: *"You had everything going for you. You were in Eden, God's garden. You were dressed in splendor, your robe studded with jewels* [then a list of the jewels found in the breastplate of the High Priest]. ... *A robe was prepared for you the same day you were created. You were the anointed cherub. I placed you on the mountain of God. You strolled in magnificence among the stones of fire. From the day of your creation you were sheer perfection ... and then imperfection—evil—was detected in you. ... I threw you, disgraced, off the mountain of God. I threw you out—you, the anointed angel-cherub. No more strolling among the gems of fire for you! Your beauty went to your head. You corrupted wisdom by using it to get worldly fame"* (Ezekiel 28:12-17).[1]

Peterson does equally well with the Isaiah passage in writing, *"What a comedown this, ... Daystar! Son of dawn! ... You said to yourself, I'll climb to heaven. I'll set my throne over the stars of God. I'll run the assembly of angels that meets on sacred Mount Zaphon. I'll climb to the top of the clouds. I'll take over as King of the Universe! But you didn't make it, did you? Instead of climbing up, you came down—down with the underground dead, down to the abyss of the Pit"* (Isaiah 14:12-16).[2]

Pride in Heaven

Pride—the curse of humanity and of angels—had to have a beginning somewhere. The locale of its beginning was Heaven, but how could something so low and vile be found in one so gifted, glorious, and glamorous? Was there a construction flaw in this creature of God's choosing? Is pride inherent to the nature of God, allowing Lucifer to learn it through observation?

The Bible doesn't even hint at the possibility of either of these two premises. God is perfect, and everything He created He pronounced "good." He could have made the angels and mankind as servile robots who were preprogramed to do His will. That would have saved Heaven and earth a great deal of trouble, but it could never have satisfied a God who is inherently "love." He has created His creatures—both angels and mankind—as free moral agents with the power of choice. God consistently wants to be loved and served by persons who desire to serve Him. He never compels us to love Him, but He lovingly challenges us to do so.

Lucifer was not created proud. However, when he began to focus on himself instead of on God the Father, something began to develop in him that had never before been experienced in Heaven. He wanted to be what God was. He tried to make himself equal with God. The creature dared to exalt himself to the status of the Creator. Lucifer began to have spiritual "I" trouble. Pride had been introduced into the lives of God's creatures, and it has not been eradicated since then, even by the sacrificial work of Christ's crucifixion.

It is in the final book of the Bible that we see how God dealt with Satan's progressive pride. We read: *"There was war in heaven. Michael and his angels fought against the dragon, and the dragon and his angels fought back. But he was not strong enough, and they lost their place in heaven. The great dragon was hurled down—that ancient serpent called the devil, or Satan, who leads the whole world astray. He was hurled to the earth, and his angels with him"* (Revelation 12:7-9, NIV).

Pride on Earth

Does it make you feel better to realize that pride had its origin in Heaven? Earth was not its source. Long before Adam was formed from the dust of the earth, pride had caused the downfall of Heaven's second highest citizen—Lucifer. When he was cast out of Heaven, it seems that the planet earth became his domain, the seat of his kingdom. It was from here that he set his sights on God's Kingdom and planned his strategy to overthrow God and replace Him completely.

It is mind-boggling to believe Lucifer could actually convince himself that he was capable of replacing God, but men on this earth think this way on a regular basis. Men of science feel that since they have discovered how God did a thing, they don't need God anymore. Religious persons have set God aside for rules, regulations, and organizations. If God dares let individuals become *"workers together with him"* (2 Corinthians 6:1), it seems an easy step to become a worker *for* Him and eventually a worker *without* Him. The more we succeed, the less we seem to feel we need God. Of course, it is not done in one easy step. Pride is progressive. Just ask Lucifer.

No one—angel or man—comes to this level of pride in one step. Isaiah suggests that there were at least five steps in the progression of

Lucifer's pride. Perhaps when Lucifer found that God didn't react with thunderbolts of judgment, he dared to take another step up in his pride. How easy it is to believe that if God's judgment isn't swift, it isn't coming. We think we are getting away with things, when God is only withholding judgment while hoping for repentance on our part. God's Word assures us: *"[The Lord] is patient with you, not wanting anyone to perish, but everyone to come to repentance"* (2 Peter 3:9, NIV).

Yes, pride was created and first exercised in Heaven—the dwelling place of the infinitely Holy One who has revealed Himself to us as — Jehovah, God Almighty. To me, this is scary! If pride could form in an atmosphere of praise, worship, purity, and ultimate spiritual power, what protection do we earthlings have against being overcome with pride? It would seem on the surface that being in the recognized presence of God would preclude the exercise of personal pride. Compared to Him, what status does any created being have?

There is a marvelous beneficence in Jehovah. He has chosen to share His glory and power with His great created beings—angels, men, and women. We often become the executors of His will and the channels through whom He ministers. Sometimes it seems that the channels take on the aura of what is flowing through them and believe that they are the power or the grace that is being transmitted through them. This makes about as much sense as for the steel pipeline to declare itself to be the gasoline that is flowing through it. Similarly, the messenger is never equal to the message or to the one who sent the message.

Pride Is a Choice

God created Lucifer with beauty and ability. He graced him with authority, skill, and position. He became a channel for God's power to flow to the attending angels, and, as such, he almost became the source of their lives. He could not help but know that he had become great in the sight of God and in the eyes of Heaven's servants, but all of this greatness was conferred—none of it was inherent to him.

Somewhere in the exercise of his office and responsibilities, Lucifer began to believe that his beauty, abilities, and authority were innate in him, that they were intrinsic to his nature. Instead of continuing to recognize that *"Every good and perfect gift is from above, coming down from the Father of the heavenly lights, who does not change like shifting shadows"* (James 1:17, NIV), Lucifer embraced the idea that he had made himself great, and that there was a possibility of achieving even more greatness. He could become like Jehovah, and maybe even become greater than God.

We have no way of knowing the time span involved in the development of this personal philosophy, for in eternity there seems to be no measurement of time. We can, nonetheless, project that it developed through a succession of choices—each one built upon the preceding choice. Since God did not prohibit choice number one, Lucifer dared to make choice number two, and so forth.

What Lucifer didn't seem to understand (and neither do we mere mortals) is that God lets us have our choices. He made each of us with the power of choice and the right to exercise that option. Although God knows the penalties attached to our choices, He will do no more than warn and inform us. He will not force us to make His choices. As Oswald Chambers puts it, "God regenerates us and puts us in contact with all his divine resources, but he cannot make us walk according to his will."[3]

As angels repeatedly brought Lucifer praise and glory to be given to the Father, Lucifer took that praise to himself. It was a deliberate decision, and God did not contest it. This made it easier for Lucifer to accept the next offering of praise as belonging to himself, and not to Father God.

Lucifer built his destructive pride upon decision after decision, and so do we! If we accept the praises of people, we will soon believe those praises and begin to function as minigods among men.

In my early traveling ministry, I was greatly disturbed by the praise given to me for my teaching ministry. I often rebuked people by telling them, "Give God the glory." In a prayer session one day, God asked me why I was so hard on His children. "They don't know how to give the glory to Me directly," He said, "but you should know how to receive it and, in turn, give it to Me. Treat each compliment as a flower. Thank them for their praises, and then put them together as a bouquet and present it to Me."

From that day to this, I have joyfully collected praise flowers. Before going to sleep at night, I present this bouquet to Father God. I have the pleasure of smelling the flowers, but He has the responsibility of handling them. This helps me keep my pride level in check. I recognize that the flowers I hold in my hand do not belong to me; I am but the floral delivery person.

This is a choice—a daily choice—but to not make this choice is to face the danger of destructive pride overwhelming me. The day I'd begin to believe all that others say about me would be the beginning of the end of my ministry.

As I watch some of the more successful ministers of our generation, successful at least in numbers and ministry schedules, I sense a rising pride that will surely spell the downfall of these ministers and their ministries. Unfortunately, just as Lucifer pulled a third of Heaven's angels down with him, many earnest believers will fall when these men fall. God, however, allows us the choice to boast and even believe we are great, but He has already explained to us what such boasting will produce.

Prayer alone, especially if it is basically a monologue, will not immunize any of us to pride. Pride is a choice we make—a choice to see ourselves as great, even though we know that all the elements that have made us extraordinary have come from God. Almost tragically, God will let us have our way. Just ask Adam and Eve.

Endnotes:

1. Eugene H. Peterson, *The Message: The Prophets* (Colorado Springs: NavPress, 2000)
2. IBID.
3. Oswald Chambers as quoted in the *Bible Illustrator for Windows, Ver. 3.0,* (Fremont, Ca.: Parsons Technology, Inc., 1990-1998)

Dear Jesus,

When I realize that pride had its origin in Heaven in the most glorious of all the angels, what chance do I have? I am a mere mortal who was born with a high level of pride. I don't want to be cast down as was Lucifer. Please help me. I know You lived a life of humility here on the earth, but I don't seem able to follow that model. Please cause your Holy Spirit to bring me beyond my pride levels to open honesty—especially with You.

Thank You, Lord.
Amen!

• • •

Questions

1. How do you handle receiving compliments? Is it difficult or easy? Why?

2. What helps you receive compliments without becoming prideful? (For example, I treat them as a bouquet of flowers to give to the Lord at the end of the day).

3. How is pride a progressive result of choices?

Part II

PORTRAITS OF PRIDE

Chapter 3

PRIDE AND OBEDIENCE

Now the serpent was more subtil than any beast ... . And he said unto the woman, ... Hath God said, Ye shall not eat of every tree of the garden? And the woman said ..., We may eat ..., but of the tree ... in the midst of the garden, God ... said, Ye shall not eat ..., neither ... touch it, lest ye die. And the serpent said ..., Ye shall not ... die: for God doth know that in the day ye eat ..., your eyes shall be opened, and ye shall be as gods. ... And when the woman saw that the tree was good for food, and ... to be desired to make one wise, she took ..., and did eat, and gave also unto her husband ... . And the eyes of them both were opened, and they knew that they were naked; and they sewed fig leaves ..., and made themselves aprons. And they heard the voice of ... God ... : and Adam and his wife hid themselves ... . And ... God called unto Adam, ... Where art thou? And he said, ... I was afraid, because I was naked ... . And he said, Who told thee ...? Hast thou eaten of the tree ...? And the man said, The woman ... gave me of the tree ... . God said unto the woman, What is this that thou hast done? And the woman said, The serpent beguiled me, and I did eat. And ... God said unto the serpent, ... Thou art cursed ...; upon thy belly shalt thou go, and dust shalt thou eat ... . And I will put enmity between thee and the woman, and between thy seed and her seed; it shall bruise thy head, and thou shalt bruise his heel. Unto the woman he said, ... In sorrow thou shalt bring forth children; and ... thy husband ... shall rule over thee. And unto Adam he said, ... Cursed is the ground for thy sake; in sorrow shalt thou eat of it ...; Thorns ... shall it bring forth ...; and thou shalt eat the herb ...; in the sweat of thy face shalt thou eat ..., till thou return unto ... dust. And Adam called his wife's name Eve; because she was the mother of all living. Unto Adam ... and ... his wife did ... God make coats of skins, and clothed them. Genesis 3:1-21

*A*ccording to *Webster's Dictionary*, *polarity* refers to at least three things: (1) Exhibition of opposite properties or powers in contrasted directions; (2) attraction toward a particular object; (3) a diametrical opposition. As we will see, pride fits all three of these definitions.

When Lucifer was lifted up in pride, he began to exhibit properties or powers in contrasted directions. He was drawing all attention away from the Father to himself in diametrical opposition to God's plans, purposes, and provisions. Like the poles of a magnet that work against one another, Satan set himself up as the competitor of God.

As I stated in Chapter 2, when Lucifer was cast out of Heaven, the planet earth became his domain—the seat of his kingdom. It was from here that he set his sights on God's domain and planned his strategy to overthrow God and replace Him completely. Not only was he cast out of Heaven, his heavenly name Lucifer was stripped from him and he was called serpent, Satan, and devil—all of which refer to his accusative nature. He is declared to be a *"deceiver"* and an *"accuser of our brethren"* (Revelation 12:9-10, NRS).

Knowing that the nature of God abhors a vacuum, Satan no doubt expected God to replace him, and probably rather quickly. He may have been surprised that neither the archangels Gabriel nor Michael was promoted to fill the spot he had vacated in Heaven. This would have been a logical choice, for Satan had been an anointed cherub, or archangel, but these two faithful and mighty servants of God already had sufficient duties to occupy them throughout eternity. Instead of promotion, God chose to create another, and very different, being to take the intimate place Satan had occupied as God's companion. The archangel was replaced by a being with a status below that of an of an angel. God made a man and a woman to have intimate relationship with Him.

Satan's Replacement Created on Earth

Through the prophet Isaiah, God said, " *'For my thoughts are not your thoughts, neither are your ways my ways'* ... . *'As the heavens are higher than the earth, so are my ways higher than your ways and my thoughts than your thoughts'* " (Isaiah 55:8-9, NIV). Since He said it, that settles it. I am not capable of understanding the thoughts of God—especially His reasoning in choosing to put man here on the earth, the seat of Satan's kingdom. Weren't there thousands of other planets that could have made a wonderful habitation for this new creature, man?

One wonders if God was just challenging Satan. When the Father took the soil of the earth that Satan claimed was his and formed Satan's replacement, was God just "rubbing it in"? Imagine Satan's acute sense of embarrassment and disappointment when Father God leaned over and breathed His very breath into this hand-molded creation and watched it become *"a living soul"* (Genesis 2:7). Later God divided this creation into man and woman and gave them the power to procreate and thus multiply themselves.

Did Satan still possess intuitive knowledge of what was on the mind of God, or did the Father send a special word to Satan, letting him know that Adam and Eve (and the multiple millions who would come from them) would become the *"bride, the Lamb's wife"* (Revelation 21:9) and the *"body of Christ"* (1 Corinthians 12:27)? These special creations were not merely archangels; they were members of Christ, indwelt with the Spirit of God. They were to become *"members of his body"* (Ephesians 5:30). They were the ultimate and absolute replacement for the fallen archangel, Lucifer.

Pride Scorned Produces Anger and Hatred

In the loneliness of his exile from God's presence, it must have been costly to Satan to watch Adam and Eve walk with and commune with God in the garden during the cool of the day. Close fellowship is seldom appreciated more than after it is lost, and that loss is magnified when we see another enjoying what we have forfeited.

To say that Satan hated Adam and Eve would be the understatement of the century. The devil had been cast out of his high position and cut off from his intimate relationship with Father God, and these lowly creatures of the dust had been elevated to fill his spot. I believe he would have destroyed them if he could have, but God places a wall of protection around those who love Him and maintain a warm fellowship with Him. Reread the book of Job for proof of this. Satan is very limited in how far he can go against's God's chosen ones.

When I was ministering in Singapore, a missionary on his way home to America told me this eyewitness story: An African businessman in a remote village accepted Jesus Christ as his personal Savior, and it so changed his lifestyle and business methods that his business partner sought out a witch doctor to have him killed. A price was agreed upon, and a time was set for this to be accomplished. The deadline came and went with no damage to the believer. When the witch doctor was confronted with the failure, he said he was experiencing unusual difficulty and needed something personal from this man. A slipper belonging to the Christian man was stolen out of his home and given to the witch doctor, who assured the partner that the demons would now be successful in slaying the Christian.

After a week, the witch doctor returned the fee he had charged, saying that every demon he sent to slay this believer declared that there was an impenetrable wall of fire around the man's home and that he could not get to him.

In speaking of Jerusalem, God told the prophet, *"For I, saith the LORD, will be unto her a wall of fire round about, and will be the glory in the midst of her"* (Zechariah 2:5). Perhaps God still builds a wall of fire around His children. I'm confident this was true of Adam and Eve in the garden. Satan couldn't touch them, no matter how jealous he had become of them.

Adam and Eve were loved by God and hated by Satan. That's the preferred arrangement.

Satan's Tactics

If Satan had nothing more than personal experience to draw upon, he would be far smarter than the wisest man. He could well say "been there, done that" to almost every life situation we face. When he recognized that he could not destroy this special creature of God's love, he reflected back on his past and realized that just as he had self-destructed, he might be able to get these people to exchange obedience to God for personal pride. At least it was worth a try.

The scriptural account of this face-to-face communication between Eve and the serpent is found in Genesis 3:1-8. In characteristic literary style, the author compresses the entire incident and presents it as though it had occurred in a single moment of time. It is far more likely to have been a progressive confrontation, for it takes pride a little while to form roots in our lives.

We are told, *"Now the serpent was more subtil [crafty, NIV] than any beast of the field which the LORD God had made. And he said unto the woman, Yea, hath God said, Ye shall not eat of every tree of the garden?"* (Genesis 3:1). Satan entered this clever beast and spoke to Eve through him. Why it did not seem strange to Eve that a reptile could speak her language, I'll never know, but Satan consistently causes people to accept virtual reality as the real thing. He loves to play mind tricks on us.

This communication, or series of communications, first questioned God's Word to them, and then dared to refute it. The serpent asked the leading question, *"Hath God said, Ye shall not eat of every tree of the garden?"* (Genesis 3:1). In answering him, Eve quoted God's prohibition of eating of the tree of the knowledge of good and evil, but she added to God's Word in saying they were also prohibited from touching it. We're already in trouble when we add to what God has said.

Pride and Obedience

This gave Satan courage to take the second step in saying, *"Ye shall not surely die"* (Genesis 3:4). He presented his word as more authoritative than God's Word. In doing this, he was making God seem like a liar. Satan's tactics have not changed to this date. First he questions God's Word and gets us to make it more severe than God made it. Then he points out how illogical God's command actually is, and dares to say God didn't really mean what He said.

This is the setup for Satan to utterly contradict God and make Him seem selfish and unkind. He told Eve, *"For God knows that when you eat of it your eyes will be opened, and you will be like God, knowing good and evil"* (Genesis 3:5, NIV). The tempter convinced Eve that God was withholding something very vital from her. This is typical. The devil consistently convinces men and women that serving God will cheat them out of the better things of life.

The *coup de grâce* was Satan's assertion that eating of the forbidden fruit would cause these special creatures to ascend in understanding to God's level of intellect. Had Eve waited until the cool of the day to discuss this with God, things would have turned out very differently. But she acted on the impulse of personal pride. "I can be like God," her emotions screamed, so she ate of the fruit and shared it with Adam.

The polarity was more than she was prepared to handle. Her pride had produced an attraction toward self-exaltation. This was in diametrical opposition to the life of obedience she had lived until this point. She was choosing her course in life, even though it was in opposition to the choice God had made for her. She had a chance to become something more than "Adam's wife," and her innate pride jumped at the chance.

Does this all seem very familiar? It should, for it is merely an adaptation of Satan's own experience with pride. Please note that Satan did not impart pride to Eve. He didn't force it upon her, nor teach it to her. He merely incited her personal pride into action against God. Satan need not give us something we do not possess. He is quite successful when toying with the pride with which we were born.

Was God shielding Adam and Eve from a knowledge of evil? Yes! All that they knew they had learned from God, and He is a good God. They didn't need to know evil, with its pain, depravation, and destruction, so God did not expose them to it. Somehow, Satan had painted evil as a beautiful experience and as a tool to make Eve godlike. He bypassed her intellect and went directly to her emotions, drawing upon her pride of being. We are never in greater danger than when we take guidance from our emotions instead of from our spirits.

Pride in Position Replaced Personal Relationship

How exhilarating it was for Adam and Eve to believe that they had become "like God." This first man and woman had learned good things from a good teacher, and it induced humility and obedience in them, but they became proud when they were introduced to intellectual knowledge and evil. Satan consistently tempts Christians to trade their intimate relationship with God for intellectual knowledge. Pride wants to know from the head; humility is content to know from the heart. This has been the curse of religion from that day to this. We think that our knowledge of God equals a relationship with Him. Pride puffs up; humility lifts up. It isn't necessary to have a doctorate to fellowship with God.

Almost immediately, Adam and Eve were expelled from the Garden of Eden. Instead of ascending to the heights to sit with God as His equals, they lost the little place where God used to come to fellowship with them face-to-face. Whereas they had added one more tree to God's food supply, they now lost all of God's supply and were told to till the soil for their food.

The desire to be like God probably stems from God breathing His very breath, the breath of life, into Adam's nostrils. There is something of the nature of God in humanity, and it cries loudly for expression and enlargement. Even the New Testament teaches us that the work of Christ at Calvary and the ministry of the Holy Spirit in us is to make us godlike. However, none of the grace of God is provided to cause us to replace God, but rather for us to become one with His moral nature. God wants to bring us into His love, joy, and peace that form the basis of His Kingdom.

Unfortunately, many of us are discontent with being transformed into the moral nature of God. From time to time God shares with us a measure of His power and wisdom, and this frequently arouses our personal pride to the point that we try to act like God.

I observe that some Christians seem to feel that they are so close to being God that they can order the Father around. I've watched many make a big production of telling God what to do and when to do it. They seem to project that they have authority over God: they give the orders, and God obeys them.

How odious can our self-serving pride become?

Dear Jesus,

I really do want my own way most of the time. I am selfish and sometimes feel that You are withholding things from me that would benefit me. Please forgive me. I know that Your ways are best. Please help me to be obedient to Your will and commands. Don't simply trust me to obey; chasten me when I disobey. I would rather have You inflict discipline in love than to continue in my proud self-will. Forgive me if I cry when You correct me, but keep doing it until I submit. I really do want to live in obedience to Your Word. It's just that my pride gets in the way.

Thank You, Lord.
Amen!

• • •

Questions

1. Some say acting like we are God is addictive. We want to be in control. Name some experiences or areas of your life where you want to be in control.

2. Do you agree that we are born with pride? Why?

3. In what areas of your life do you need to let God be God?

4. What are some examples of how a person acts like God?

Chapter 4

PRIDE AND WORSHIP

Adam lay with his wife Eve, and she became pregnant and gave birth to Cain. She said, "With the help of the LORD I have brought forth a man." Later she gave birth to his brother Abel. Now Abel kept flocks, and Cain worked the soil. In the course of time Cain brought some of the fruits of the soil as an offering to the LORD. But Abel brought fat portions from some of the firstborn of his flock. The LORD looked with favor on Abel and his offering, but on Cain and his offering he did not look with favor. So Cain was very angry, and his face was downcast.

Then the LORD said to Cain, "Why are you angry? Why is your face downcast? If you do what is right, will you not be accepted? But if you do not do what is right, sin is crouching at your door; it desires to have you, but you must master it."

Now Cain said to his brother Abel, "Let's go out to the field." And while they were in the field, Cain attacked his brother Abel and killed him.

Then the LORD said to Cain, "Where is your brother Abel?"

"I don't know," he replied. "Am I my brother's keeper?"

The LORD said, "What have you done? Listen! Your brother's blood cries out to me from the ground. Now you are under a curse and driven from the ground, which opened its mouth to receive your brother's blood from your hand. When you work the ground, it will no longer yield its crops for you. You will be a restless wanderer on the earth."

Cain said to the LORD, "My punishment is more than I can bear. Today you are driving me from the land, and I will be hidden from your presence; I will be a restless wanderer on the earth, and whoever finds me will kill me."

But the LORD said to him, "Not so; if anyone kills Cain, he will suffer vengeance seven times over." Then the LORD put a mark on Cain so that no one who found him would kill him.

Genesis 4:1-15, NIV

*J*ust as I stand in awe at the forcefulness of the wind, I am equally unable to comprehend the power of choice. In the Garden of Eden, God tested His first man and woman in the area of obedience, and they failed the test miserably. To say that they were punished for this disobedience may be an overstatement. God had allowed them a choice, and that choice became a detour from the will of God. Their choice brought expulsion from the Garden of Eden and all of its provisions. Was this punishment or was it merely the natural result of their choice? As it developed, that was punishment enough. When God lets us have our own way, it is usually all the punishment we need.

Before the exile of Adam and Eve from the Garden of Eden, God provided them with a means to approach Him—through sacrifice. He understands far better than we do how vital it is that we worship Him. He is the Source of our life, and worship is our contact with Him. To be cut off from worship is to be sentenced to spiritual death.

Adam and Eve lived under a canopy of divine grace in their new habitat. By Genesis 4, they seem to have been animated by hope, assured of the divine forgiveness and filled with a sweet peace. They set up housekeeping and began to raise a family.

We can certainly wonder how different the human race might have been if the first son of Adam and Eve had been born in the garden before their rebellion. Cain came into the family after their exile.

Unfortunately, Cain was born with a fallen nature, not a sinless one. Mercifully, this son came to a forgiven couple who were looking for a promised Redeemer. Many Bible commentators suggest that Eve saw Cain as the Redeemer. Wouldn't we expect Adam and Eve to give this first son ample spiritual training? Surely they didn't want him to make the same mistake they had made. Quite likely, they shared with their sons all the spiritual training they had received from God before their exile. If a person could be trained to be spiritual, Cain should have been a very spiritual person.

Just as we parents want our children to be like us, these first parents probably expected their sons to be clones of themselves. Imagine their pain when they discovered what we have also learned: our children usually duplicate our worst traits. No matter how much Eve may have taught her sons about the danger of pride, Cain became a man driven by this evil force. His natural disposition overrode his intellectual training.

Cain's Pride Offered a Substitute for God's Order of Worship

You do not need to serve the Lord very long to discover that all training will be tested. While his parents had been tested in the area of obedience, Cain was tested in the area of his worship. We read, *"In process of time it came to pass, that Cain brought of the fruit of the ground an offering unto the LORD"* (Genesis 4:3). What this *"course of time"* might have been, the Bible does not say, but it seems safe to assume that either God or Adam had established a place, a pattern, and a time for worship. We may presume that the place of worship was east of the garden where God had stationed cherubim and a flaming sword to guard the way to the tree of life.

One day at worship time, Cain faced his first major test. He had learned from his parents the importance of obedience, so he showed up at the right time and place for worship, to offer a sacrifice unto God. Unfortunately, Cain's pride consistently got in the way of his worship, much as it had with Lucifer in Heaven and with Eve in the garden.

Cain was the farmer in the family, so he naturally brought some of his produce when he came to worship. This may seem to be very logical, and later, in the Mosaic Law, God provided for His people to bring the produce of the land to the priests as a thank offering to God in the harvest season. However, fruits and vegetables could never be used as substitutes for a blood sacrifice. From God's slaying of animals in the Garden of Eden to the substitutionary death of Jesus on Calvary, it has always been the shedding of blood that makes atonement for sin. No other substitute has ever been accepted by God.

Cain bypassed God's prescribed way of worship by substituting his own form of sacrifice. He thought he was improving on God's system. He had chosen to worship God in his own way, for it was more convenient. What pride!

Cain did not raise animals, but he had some of the finest produce in the land. He wanted to present, in his public worship, the bountiful work of his hands. He was the forerunner of those rich persons Jesus spoke of who had trumpeters go before them to draw attention to the gifts that were being brought into the temple.

True worshipers of God will not draw attention to themselves. They have come to a place of worship to deal with God, and they have discovered that submission to God, not display of self, is the heart of worship. Cain had learned from his parents the terrible consequence of disobedience, so he obediently came to the place of worship at the time of worship and with a desire to worship God. Unfortunately, his pride kept him from worshiping God the way God wanted to be worshiped.

This is quite consistent with many of the attendees in the Sunday morning services in many of our churches. Not all who are present are true worshipers of God. Some have come because it is a custom to go to church on Sunday morning. Others come to church because they feel that they must pay some attention to social propriety and conscience. Still others come for business reasons. They are present, but don't expect them to praise, pray, or even participate in the offering. They may display some talent if given a chance, but it will be designed to draw attention to themselves rather than to glorify God. Their personal pride will not allow them to raise their hands to God nor to bend their knees in His presence.

Cain's Pride Was Stingy

Not only did Cain bring produce instead of an animal for a sacrifice, but he was stingy with what he brought to God. It is reported that he brought of the *"some of the fruits,"* not all—suggesting that he brought one or two items from his harvest. Perhaps he had raised an oversized pumpkin or radish that he felt needed to be put on display, and God's altar seemed to be a good place to do this.

Like Cain in the Old Testament, many people will go through a form of worship as long as they can design that form. Don't expect it to involve very much sacrifice. If our hearts are not surrendered to God, it is very unlikely that our wallets and bank accounts will be given to Him.

It is almost universally true that when we choose to worship God our way rather than the way God has revealed He wants to be worshiped, we tend to be tightfisted with God. Many are the well-dressed Sunday morning church attendees who arrived in luxury automobiles and reluctantly drop a dollar bill into the offering plate. This is their maximum offering to God, and they would rather die than pay God the tithe that is due Him. This seems to have been Cain's prideful attitude.

It is so easy to be stingy with our worship. Some churches schedule barely ten minutes of the Sunday morning service for participation in worship. In congregations that budget a lengthy season for vocal and musical worship, some members deliberately come late for the service in order to miss much of the worship session. They are stingy with their worship. They are willing to give God one or two songs, but that is all. How proud can we get? God has given us one hundred and sixty-eight hours each week. Why are we so stingy with the amount of that time we give back to Him in worship?

Cain's Pride Excluded Faith

The Genesis account contrasts the sacrifices of Cain and Abel, and puts great emphasis on Abel's sacrifice of an animal to God. Abel gave to God what God had requested, and both Abel and his sacrifice were accepted and blessed by God. It isn't until we get to the book of Hebrews that we discover another great contrast in the worship of these two sons. This New Testament writer says, *"By faith Abel offered God a better sacrifice than Cain did. By faith he was commended as a righteous man, when God spoke well of his offerings"* (Hebrews 11:4, NIV).

Not only did Abel offer God a better sacrifice, he offered it in a better manner. He mixed his worship with faith in God and in His provision. Abel believed that if he would do what God told him to do, God would do what He had promised to do. This entire eleventh chapter of Hebrews emphasizes the value God places on faith. It even goes so far as to say, *"Without faith it is impossible to please God, because anyone who comes to him must believe that he exists and that he rewards those who earnestly seek him"* (Hebrews 11:6, NIV).

Pride and faith are opposites. They are as far removed from one another as the North Pole is distant from the South Pole. They will never get together. Pride produces self-reliance, while the heart of faith is God-reliance. Faith says, "I believe God can." Pride says, "I believe I can." Cain pridefully set himself up as an authority on worship. He was convinced that his way was ideal. However, while it may have looked good, it failed to gain God's acceptance.

As long as we are exalting ourselves in prayer, we do not need faith, but when we reach out to God for His intervention in our affairs, we need much faith. Abel seemed to have this faith, while Cain tried to worship without it. He tried to get by on his good works.

Are we not often guilty of the same sin? When will we learn that no amount of singing, shouting, dancing, or praying will be accepted as divine worship unless it is offered in faith. Performance and ritual are not what God desires. He longs for persons who will set aside their pride and worship him *"in spirit and in truth"* (John 4:24).

Cain's Pride Sought Self-sufficiency

There is no reason to believe this was Cain's first worship experience. As a young boy in the home, he had undoubtedly joined his father at an altar as sacrifice was made unto God. He knew that Jehovah required the shedding of blood for worship to be acceptable to Him, but this posed a problem for Cain. It meant that he would have to secure a lamb from his shepherd brother. In his pride of independence, Cain was unwilling to ask Abel for help.

Things haven't changed much, have they? Many persons do not want to be dependent upon the worship leaders in the church. They declare that they can worship God just as well in the home as in the church. They state that they get as much out of private reading of the Bible as in listening to the pastor preach. They do not want to be dependent upon the ministries of others to lead them in their approach to God.

Having sat on the platforms of many hundreds of churches across this nation during their worship sessions, I have observed that many persons choose their own patterns of worship. They have silent prayer while the congregation is singing. Many sit and read their Bibles while others stand with their hands raised in praise to God. They will not go to "Abel" to get what is needed for that day's worship. Pride always tells us that our way is best. It frequently points to our current feelings. True worshipers control their feelings rather than allow themselves to be controlled by those feelings. By an act of our will, we can participate in any form of worship that is being led ... that is, unless our pride is in control of our worship.

Cain's Pride Generated Jealousy and Anger

It seems incongruous for Cain to be jealous and angry at the place of worship, but when God accepted Abel's offering and blessed him, it threw Cain into a jealous rage. When pride reigns during the worship session, jealousy stands at attention waiting to become active. It has long been said that the music department is the war department of the church. Instead of completion, there is often competition among the musicians. Every music director can share stories of persons who walked out of the service because they did not get to sing the solo part they wanted.

Of course it is not only the musicians who let jealousy pull their attention away from God. I have watched pastors take the worship session away from the worship leader because it seemed to be getting out of control. It was not following the printed schedule. Or maybe the leader was succeeding too well. Perhaps too much attention was being given to Jesus, and the pastor felt jealous.

This same worship jealousy can be seen in the congregation. If some members of the congregation seemed to touch Christ in worship, others react in jealousy and become critical. Instead of rejoicing with those who were caught up in a worship experience, some people take it as a personal rejection that they have not entered that realm. Nothing can trigger religious rage faster than to feel that God has accepted one brother or sister and rejected another.

Lately, God has been visiting separate congregations here in the United States by giving them a measure of revival. This has caused many persons to visit these places and get a touch of God on their own lives. Far more persons, however, seem to become critical with the way God is manifesting Himself. Some have even dared to declare that if there was a genuine visitation of God, it would have come to their church. This sounds to me like spiritual pride exploding in jealousy. Perhaps we need to hear again what God told Cain: *"If you do what is right, will you not be accepted? But if you do not do what is right, sin is crouching at your door; it desires to have you, but you must master it"* (Genesis 4:7, NIV).

Cain's Pride Grew Into Murderous Rage

How tragic that Cain murdered his brother Abel over this worship experience! How I wish that this was the last time this ever happened, but I have watched it repeated over the years. It is seldom done with a knife or a gun. It is usually done with the tongue. Many a pastor's ministry has been destroyed by false accusations from the congregation that were actually rooted in pride. Similarly, persons with a musical praise ministry have been killed by unkind criticism.

Jesus taught that murder does not begin with a blow to the head, but with an attitude of the heart. He says that to hate our brother is equal to killing him. How important it becomes, then, to guard our pride during times of worship. If that worship turns our attention inward, we will be subject to jealousy that can so easily lead to murder.

As a result of this action, Cain was expelled from the family and from the place of worship. This is what happened to Lucifer in Heaven and to Eve in the garden. When pride rears its ugly head in times of worship, we will find ourselves shut off from the presence of God and exiled from worship. If we have felt that we could worship without God, God says, "Be My guest." Once again, He lets us have our own way, but the results are not pleasant.

Pride and Worship

The rest of Genesis 4 shows us how miserable Cain's own way became for him and for the generations that followed him. How tragic it is that our decisions affect not only ourselves, but our children and our children's children!

Dear Heavenly Father,

I thank You for putting a desire, even a need, in my heart to worship You. There are times when worship is the most glorious thing I can do. There are other times, Lord, when my pride gets in the way and draws attention that belongs to You to myself. Sometimes I want to worship You my way, even though I know that I must worship Your revealed way. Forgive me for this selfish thinking that I could improve on Your way. I really do want to be a true worshiper of You. Thank You for the help of Your Holy Spirit that You have given to me.

I love You, Lord.
Amen!

• • •

Questions

1. I have said that our children duplicate our worst traits. How is this true in your family? What personal traits do you see in your children?

2. How does pride hinder you from worshiping God?

3. Pride produces self-reliance. In what area do you need grace to rely on God?

4. What worship style is easiest for you to enter into God's presence?

5. How has being critical of the worship of others hindered you from participating?

Chapter 5

PRIDE AND TECHNOLOGY

Now the whole world had one language and a common speech. As men moved eastward, they found a plain in Shinar and settled there.

They said to each other, "Come, let's make bricks and bake them thoroughly." They used brick instead of stone, and tar for mortar. Then they said, "Come, let us build ourselves a city, with a tower that reaches to the heavens, so that we may make a name for ourselves and not be scattered over the face of the whole earth."

But the LORD came down to see the city and the tower that the men were building. The LORD said, "If as one people speaking the same language they have begun to do this, then nothing they plan to do will be impossible for them. Come, let us go down and confuse their language so they will not understand each other." So the LORD scattered them from there over all the earth, and they stopped building the city. That is why it was called Babel—because there the LORD confused the language of the whole world. From there the LORD scattered them over the face of the whole earth. Genesis 11:1-9, NIV

*I*n these early portraits of pride, we have seen that pride separates the proud from the presence of God and thus violates God's purpose for the creation of man and woman. Mercifully, God has consistently provided a way back into His presence, for He loves to fellowship with mankind. God demonstrated to Adam the way to offer a sacrifice. He must have further communicated this to Cain and Abel, for Abel offered his sacrifice in faith, and *"faith comes by hearing, and hearing by the word of God"* (Romans 10:17).

Cain heard, but he did not believe what he heard. He invented what he must have supposed to be a better or more excellent way. He offered to God the fruit from the very ground that God had cursed. He offered to God the "sweat of his brow" rather than the "blood of the lamb." E.W. Bullinger declares, "The way of Cain was the first step in the evolution of religion. Its developments and ramifications are today innumerable."[1]

Just as Cain seemed to be unwilling or unable to believe that God had done everything necessary to bring him back into fellowship with Himself, so succeeding generations of people have consistently believed that they had to "do" something to make access to God available. This "doing" became so evil that God regretted having made man, and He sent the flood to destroy all but the family of Noah.

Genesis Chapter 10 is a list of the descendants of Noah and his sons. When we come to Chapter 11, we discover that God's severe judgment had not destroyed the native pride that is in every person. Many of these descendants came to a plain in Shinar, and there they said, *"Come, let us build ourselves a city, with a tower that reaches to the heavens, SO THAT WE MAY MAKE A NAME FOR OURSELVES and not be scattered over the face of the whole earth"* (Genesis 11:4, NIV). This so displeased God that He confounded their language and scattered them across the earth.

The Illustrated Bible Dictionary says, "Babel thus becomes a synonym for the confusion caused by language differences which was part of the divine punishment for the human pride displayed in the building."[2] What was the basis for this "human pride displayed in the building"? *"They said to each other, 'Come, let's make bricks and bake them thoroughly.' They used brick instead of stone, and tar for mortar"* (Genesis 11:3, NIV). They had developed a new technology. Archaeologists confirm that there is no stone available in the plain of Shinar. Someone in that particular generation had discovered how to make a substitute for stone and how to mortar the resulting blocks or bricks together with bitumen (which was probably floated down the Euphrates River from Hit).

This new technology proved to be very good. Some of the towers built with these bricks more than five hundred years before Christ are still standing. There was nothing wrong with the technology, but trying to use bricks to bring them to God (if, in fact, that was the purpose of the tower) only further separated the people of Babel from God. Once again, we find men pridefully trying to "do" something to come into God's presence rather than to believe that God has made His presence available through the blood sacrifice that looked forward to the cross of Jesus.

The technology of today's generation has placed men on the moon, has landed a vehicle on Mars, and may very well scoff at the technology of brick making, but the development of technology is progressive. This early civilization had made a significant breakthrough, and they were very proud of it.

As I write this, I am in my late seventies. In my lifetime, I have seen an amazing amount of technological development. In transportation, we've come from the horse and buggy to the jet airplane. In communication, we have moved from one telephone in a neighborhood to cell phones owned by almost everyone and radios everywhere. When

Pride and Technology

I went to school, we still had inkwells in our desks, and we learned penmanship. Now we have people who have never even seen a typewriter, and yet they are very computer literate. Television lets us see all around the world and has exposed us to a great variety of cultures. Knowledge has increased at such a rapid rate that no one can keep up with it.

This has brought about amazing changes in our living. Unfortunately, it has also brought about changes in our worship patterns. This is a generation that worships science. Our technology has become our god. We may not be building towers to reach God, but we have developed a civilization that does not recognize a need for God. Christians in America are considered a minority group. America's faith is in what we can "do." Our pride in our accomplishments fills the television screen every night.

This would be serious if it were only true culturally. Unfortunately, however, it is also true spiritually. Our churches in America are very high-tech, and often our pride in our technology exceeds our pride in God. Often the public address system in a new church costs multiple thousands of dollars. Giant television screens give the congregation a better view of the pulpit activities. We have overhead projectors, wireless microphones, television cameras, and prerecorded music and sound tracks. We use tape recorders and duplicators to make copies of the sermon available almost instantly. No generation has had more high-tech tools available to help spread the Gospel. But are we doing a better job with all these tools? Sometimes and in some places we are. At other times and in other places I get the feeling that the church members are deeply proud that they are as high-tech as the world, but their message gets lost in the tools they are using.

I have visited many of the great cathedrals of Europe, and I have preached in several of them. They are great monuments to the skillful work of generations of artisans who sacrificed their lives to satisfy the pride of a religious organization. These workers were told that what they did was "to the glory of God," but it was actually often for the glory of man.

Many congregations have been plunged into multi-million-dollar debt to finance a new church structure they really didn't need, only because their pastor wanted to make a name for himself—his pride being the controlling factor. His fellow pastors had built new structures, and he felt he must keep up with them or exceed them.

Of course, congregations need a place to assemble, and it is a great convenience if they can have their own facility. I have led two congregations in building a worship facility. God is not displeased when churches are built, but since God is unchangeable, I can't help but believe He is unhappy when the motive for the elaborate structures we have erected in His name has been pride, or wanting to make a name for ourselves. After all, that was the sin for which Babel was judged.

I am aware that religion has consistently resisted change and has often denounced new technology. As a boy, I remember hearing campmeeting speakers denounce the radio as "the devil's box," and they suggested that owning one would put our salvation in jeopardy. The same would be said of television when it became available.

The church has slowly come to see that technology is amoral—neither good nor bad. We have learned to use the tools of radio, television, telephones, and computers to spread the Gospel in all areas of the world. These same technologies are being used by the enemy to subvert the minds of men and women from the grace of the Gospel. It is not the tool, but the hand that uses the tool that determines what is produced.

Remember, these people on the Shinar plain were not condemned for making bricks or for building a city. It was their extreme pride motivation that so displeased God and caused Him to intervene with such severity. Everything they did was to call attention to themselves. They wanted to make a name for themselves.

Actually, this sounds quite current, doesn't it? So much of our religious activity seems to have a similar desire: "Look at me." A large percentage of what we call "Christian" television is little more than second- or third-rate entertainment. We parade personality after personality across the screen as they tell us how great they are or how great their ministry has become. It is not too unusual to have to listen to several successive broadcasts to hear about Jesus and His Gospel. We've learned to use this communications technology to build a name for ourselves.

Some local churches have recognized the power of television as a means of mass communication. They have invested great sums of money in cameras and related equipment to enable them to broadcast their Sunday morning services to the shut-ins of the community, and as an evangelistic outreach to the community. Many churches do this very well, but some pastors are willing to sacrifice the worship of the local congregation for the sake of their telecast. When they begin their taping or a live broadcast, attention is drawn from Jesus to the "invisible audience." People become more aware of cameras moving around the auditorium than they are aware of the Holy Spirit's presence. The mood of the service shifts from praise to performance, from involvement with God to involvement with a telecast. The medium becomes more important than the message.

This great technology called television, this modern "brick," can become a great pride producer. It is not the only modern technology to accomplish this. Knowing that I am an avid computer user, I have had persons brag about the latest Bible program they have on their computers. When I asked for a demonstration, they had to admit they didn't know how to use it. They had never used it. Possession of the program gives them bragging rights, but it has not brought them one bit closer to God.

The same is true with Christian CDs and the various pieces of equipment used for playing them. Some persons are proud of the compact size of their portable players, while others brag about their studio sound with subwoofers and multiple speakers. They can tell you how many watts of output their amplifiers produce, but they can't tell you much about the music that is played through it. They are very proud of their "bricks," but the tower they are building with those bricks will not bring them into God's presence, for their pride is getting in the way. By having more than others, they "make a name for themselves."

As I write this chapter, I am in a lovely suite of rooms in a Victorian inn in the heart of Fairhope, Alabama. To my immediate right is a beautiful fireplace with a marble mantel, a tile hearth, a brick firebox, and ceramic logs on an iron grate. There is a framed picture of a floral bouquet over the mantel with a very tiny sign directly under the picture that says, "This fireplace is not operational." How similar to many of our churches. We have the latest equipment, the finest programs, modern technology, and great acceptance in the community, but we are "not operational." We don't seem to get the job done. We project the ability to create a fire, but it is only a facade. We have an image without life.

In his short New Testament book, the apostle Jude gives six negative analogies to persons who have *"taken the way of Cain"* (Jude 11). He writes: *"These men are blemishes at your love feasts, eating with you without the slightest qualm—shepherds who feed only themselves. They are clouds without rain, blown along by the wind; autumn trees, without fruit and uprooted—twice dead. They are wild waves of the sea, foaming up their shame; wandering stars, for whom blackest darkness has been reserved forever"* (Jude 12-13, NIV).

"The way of Cain"—doing things my way rather than God's way—is always fruitless and unproductive, although it may present a beautiful front. I have been a participant in my share of great citywide crusades, and have observed many others in which I did not participate. Massed choirs are assembled and rehearsed. Outstanding speakers are called in, and radio and television coverage is secured. It would seem that the whole city would soon be converted, for great new bricks are being used to build a tower.

Usually the attendees at such events are members of local churches who have been urged to "support" the crusade. Only seldom is the community itself affected. Although thousands of man-hours are invested in the program and great sums of money are raised to pay the bills, results are often negligible. It is a valiant attempt to "do something" to win the lost, but it often turns out to be Cain's substitute sacrifice or a tower of Babel attempt to help people reach God. We have certainly made a name for ourselves and paraded our latest technology, but our nets have too often remained empty.

Perhaps God's way is too simple for today's sophisticated generation, or is it too costly? The Bible still says: *"If my people, which are called by my name, shall humble themselves, and pray, and seek my face, and turn from their wicked ways; then will I hear from heaven, and will forgive their sin, and will heal their land"* (2 Chronicles 7:14). Why do we prefer to make bricks, burn them with fire, and construct towers trying to get people to God, when God has so clearly shown His pattern for revival?

Some of the greatest revivals the world has known came before the technology of our present generation. The meeting place was often an open field. The means of transportation was riding horses or walking. There were no overhead projectors, no public address systems, no keyboards, and no plush seating, but the presence of God was apparent. These revivals were not "produced," they were prayed into being. In them, people by the thousands accepted Jesus as their Savior. Lives were changed. Communities were revolutionized. Godliness became an accepted norm. Thus, society was positively affected.

Obviously, there is no more virtue in worshiping God in an open field than in an auditorium. Thank God for sound systems and musicians with their modern instruments. I join those who rejoice in our rapid means of communication that can let the entire world know in an instant what is happening in our services, but is anything happening that affects the Kingdom of God? Are souls being born again or merely made more comfortable in our services? Perhaps the people have come to see our brick tower more than to see our blessed God.

Is it possible that bricks are all we have on display? If this is so, it is little wonder that we are so proud of them. Cain was proud of his substitute sacrifice. The inhabitants of Shinar were proud of their brick city and tower, and we tend to be extremely proud of our technology. Oh, that we could be proud of our God again!

Endnotes:

1. E.W. Bullinger, *Great Cloud of Witnesses in Hebrews Eleven* (Grand Rapids, Mich.: Kregel Publications, 1979), p.33.
2. *The Illustrated Bible Dictionary*, Vol. I, (Wheaton, Il.: Tyndall House Publishers, 1980), pp.154-155.

Dear Father,

The world is changing too fast for me. I can't keep up. I find myself becoming lazy with the new labor-saving technology available to me. When I bring that into my relationship with You and depend on technology instead of on Your Spirit, I get into all kinds of trouble. Please help me to be simple in my walk with You. Your way may seem outdated, but it works. Help me to be childlike enough to use Your tools and Your methods in doing Your work.

Thank You.
Amen!

• • •

Questions

1. Do an experiment. Fast from watching TV, using your computer or another favorite technology, and journal your thoughts and feelings as you do. Is there an overdependence in your life on something other than God? Does that "something" separate you from God's presence?

2. How important is looking good for you? In what areas are you tempted to spend too much time and effort to look good? Is there a need for repentance in this area?

Chapter 6

PRIDE AND PANTOMIME

And Isaac entreated the LORD *for his wife, because she was barren ..., and Rebekah ... conceived. And the children struggled ... within her; and she said, ... Why am I thus? ... And the* LORD *said ..., Two nations are in thy womb, ... and the elder shall serve the younger.*

And ... there were twins in her womb. And the first came out red, ... and they called his name Esau. And after that came his brother out, and his hand took hold on Esau's heel; and his name was called Jacob. ... Esau was a cunning hunter, ... and Jacob was a plain man ... . And Isaac loved Esau ..., but Rebekah loved Jacob.

And Jacob sod pottage: and Esau came from the field, and he was faint: and Esau said to Jacob, Feed me ... that ... pottage; for I am faint ... . And Jacob said, Sell me ... thy birthright. And Esau said, ... I am at the point to die: and what profit shall this birthright do to me? ... And he sold his birthright unto Jacob. ... Thus Esau despised his birthright.

Genesis 25:21-34

And ... when Isaac was old, ... so that he could not see, he called Esau ... and said ..., I know not the day of my death: ... go out to the field, and take me some venison; and make me savoury meat ... that I may eat; that my soul may bless thee before I die. And Rebekah heard ... .

And Rebekah spake unto Jacob ..., Obey my voice ... . And his mother made savoury meat ... and ... took ... raiment of ... Esau ... and put them upon Jacob ... . And she put the skins of the kids of the goats upon his hands, and ... neck... .

And he came unto his father, and said, My father: and he said, ... Who art thou ...? And Jacob said ..., I am Esau ...; arise ..., and eat of my venison, that thy soul may bless me. ... So he blessed him.

Genesis 27:1-23

7 t is sad—almost tragic—that Jacob did not know that the believer who is ambitious to be a star disqualifies himself as a leader. It is unlikely that any other person in the Bible had a stronger drive to be number one than Jacob did.

Jacob was one of the twin sons born to Isaac and Rebecca. Although of stronger personality than his brother Esau, Jacob came out of the womb second. Even then, however, with his hand he was grasping the heel of Esau, as though he was already fighting to become the number one son. It seems that from the day of his birth, Jacob lusted to be first in the family.

These two sons could hardly have been more different. Esau was a hunter, while Jacob was a shepherd. Esau was red and hairy, but Jacob was smooth and fair. There was really no basis for competition between the two, but because Esau was born a few minutes before Jacob, Esau had the birthright of the firstborn, and Jacob, in his pride, coveted it and schemed to get it.

I never cease to be amazed at how low proud persons will stoop to get their own way. Like the pantomime actor, who turns his back to the audience to become a different character when he turns back around, these proud persons will play whatever role is necessary to achieve their goal of being number one. It doesn't matter to them how many times that role must change. They'll present themselves in any way necessary to come out on top.

Jacob was a pantomime artist. He was tremendously ambitious, but his ambition was out of control. It is likely that his doting mother had told him of the prophetic word that had come at the birth of the twins.

God had declared that the elder son would serve the younger one. Although this was a divine decree, it seems that Jacob set out to fulfill it in his own way. His pride said, "I can achieve it!"

My pastor and brother, Dr. Jim Cornwall, tells his congregation at Scottsdale Worship Center in Scottsdale, Arizona: "Pride is an unwillingness to be known as you really are. Humility is a willingness to be known as you really are." Jacob was unwilling to be known as he really was—the younger son, the second-born. His ambition led him to an attempt to change this image.

Jacob was wise enough to refrain from a frontal attack against Esau, as Cain had launched against Abel. Instead, Jacob played whatever role it took to gain the birthright.

One day Esau came in from an unsuccessful hunt, exhausted and famished. Jacob played the role of a brotherly benefactor and offered to share some of his lamb stew with his brother—for a price. Esau sold his birthright to Jacob for a bowl of stew. Later, when the pangs of hunger were gone and his exhaustion had given way to rest, Esau realized what had happened and unsuccessfully begged Jacob to give the birthright back, but Jacob was not about to return what he had coveted from childhood.

William Hazlitt wrote: "We all wear some disguise, make some professions, use some artifice, to set ourselves off as being better than we are; and yet it is not denied that we have some good intentions and praiseworthy qualities at bottom."[1] Jacob was not all bad; he was just fundamentally ambitious and willing to do anything to fulfill his ambitions. He was determined to climb the ladder of success, no matter who he had to step on to rise one rung higher.

No amount of tears and pleading could cause Jacob to return the purchased birthright to Esau. Actually, rather than return the birthright to the rightful heir, Jacob and his mother began to scheme to also cheat Esau out of the traditional blessing that fathers gave to their firstborn before dying. The charade these two played to convince Isaac that Jacob was Esau would do credit to a stage production. Taking advantage of Isaac's blindness, Rebecca covered Jacob's arms with the skins of animals so he would seem to be hairy, and had him wear one of Esau's coats so he would smell like the firstborn son. Then Jacob brought in lamb stew and presented it to his father as the venison stew Isaac had asked Esau to bring.

Although Jacob could not alter his voice to sound like Esau, he convinced his father that he was, indeed, his firstborn son, and Isaac pronounced upon him the blessing that belonged to the firstborn. Jacob seemed to achieve through deception what God had promised prophetically.

Later, when Jacob was fleeing to Padan-aram in search of a wife, he had an amazing dream of a ladder suspended between earth and Heaven, with angels ascending and descending on the ladder. In this confrontation, God greatly enlarged the blessing given to Jacob and added: *"And, behold, I am with thee, and will keep thee in all places whither thou goest, and will bring thee again into this land; for I will not leave thee, until I have done that which I have spoken to thee of"* (Genesis 28:15). God affirmed that whatever He said, He would perform. He did not need Jacob's scheming help and assistance.

How difficult this is for any of us to really believe. We feel it necessary to assist God in fulfilling a prophetic word He may give, instead of waiting for God to do what He said He would do. Our pride wants instant results, but God is not in a hurry. Sometimes it seems that God waits until our pride has died before He brings to pass what prompted that pride. There have been times when other people have had to remind me that God had proclaimed years before what was now happening in the present. I had forgotten the word, but I was enjoying the work of God when it was His time for fulfillment.

It is noteworthy to remember that Jacob received his father's blessing but lost his father's presence, for he had to flee from the wrath of Esau and never saw his father again. One wonders if the blessing was worth the cost. How tragic it would be to grasp at the promises and blessings of God, but lose the presence of God! It appears that this is happening to more and more ministers. As they strive to climb higher and higher in ministry, they walk farther and farther away from the presence of God the Father. They may be busily fulfilling His commission, but they are doing it *for* God, rather than *with* God. That's not a very good trade-off!

Jacob was discontent with the blessing of being number two; he wanted his brother's blessing. Each of us has received a blessing from the Lord. Paul taught that the Holy Spirit divides His gifts to individuals as He, the Spirit, chooses (see 1 Corinthians 12:11). We do not need to steal another's blessing or gifting, but pride often causes us to attempt to do just that.

Some years ago, there was strong competition between Christian television networks. The director of the number one network that had reached far beyond the borders of the United States was caught in a moral indiscretion. Almost immediately, the director of a smaller television ministry flew to his side, rushed him out of state, and pretended to be his benefactor and protector. He played his role so well that, far more rapidly than any of us could realize, he had gained complete control of this larger ministry. In his prideful desire to be number one, he had pulled "a Jacob" and had stolen his brother's ministry.

Amazingly, within two months, this same scene was repeated in two other television ministries in a different geographic area. Both thieving men played the actor and stole from their brothers a God-given ministry in order to enlarge their own outreach. In the process, they destroyed the ministry of another to enhance their own. Isn't it fundamental to Scripture that if we have to steal something, we actually have no right to it? Jacob, in his pride, ignored this fundamental fact, and so do many Christians today.

This same charade is played out on a daily basis in our churches. I have watched persons ambitious for position in the church play the role of an earnest prayer warrior just to get "inside information" on weaknesses in the lives of those whom they desire to replace. In feigned compassion, they talk tenderly and seemingly pray earnestly with the person until they have sufficient information to spring the trap and dispense with their "competitor."

Many pastor's wives can testify of women in the congregation who pretended to be their closest friend, but whose ultimate goal was to get close enough to the pastor to seduce him. Some have merely wanted to destroy the pastor's ministry, while others have wanted to replace the pastor's wife. They played the Jacob role and pantomimed their way to achieve the goals the pride in their hearts had produced.

God was prepared to bring Jacob into most of what he had achieved, but Jacob's pride couldn't wait for God's time. Pride seeks to accomplish in our *now* what God has scheduled for our *future*. In His ultimate wisdom, God first makes us certain promises; then He prepares us to walk and live in those promises before He actually gives us what is promised. Very seldom are we ready to receive God's promises, promotions, or even His blessings when He first tells us of them. He has to mature us to be able to walk in His provisions. Pride likes to declare that we are ready, but God knows that as long as pride speaks, the heart is not ready for greater things.

Jacob learned the hard way that using deceit to meet pride levels exposes one to greater deceit from others. He had years of deceit to deal with in his Uncle Laban. Jacob served Laban seven years to have Rachel for his wife, but he was deceived by Laban when he gave him Leah as a wife instead of Rachel. Later, Jacob charged Laban with changing his wages ten times, and there is no indication that any of these changes were a raise or a promotion. Jacob, whose name means "a supplanter, one who trips up (another)" found himself vulnerable to the same kind of treatment from others. This is another example of "What goes around, comes around." Christians who cheat to get a position live in constant fear of being cheated out of that position. It seems that there is always someone more clever at pantomime than we are.

Eventually, Jacob had enough of his father-in-law's cheating ways and headed home with his wives, children, servants, flocks, and herds. At a place Jacob later called Peniel, God confronted Jacob. All Jacob's family, flocks, and servants had gone over the river to meet Esau, and Jacob was left alone with God. The Genesis account says, *"There wrestled a man with him until the breaking of the day"* (Genesis 32:24).

Jacob declared that he was wrestling with God, but in Hosea 12:4 this "man" is called an angel.

In this confrontation, Jacob, who had seen God fulfill much of what had been promised, declared that he would not let go of his wrestling hold until the angel blessed him. He was going to have his own way with God—even if it killed him. Instead of trusting and believing God to do what He had promised, Jacob was going to wrest a blessing from God. (Are we guilty of the same error?)

Jacob was still a very proud man. God let him win this wrestling match, but he remained a cripple for the rest of his life.

God's purpose in this match was far different from Jacob's. Arthur W. Pink says, "The man was wrestling with Jacob to gain something from him—it was to reduce Jacob to a sense of his nothingness, to cause him to see what a poor, hopeless, and worthless creature he was."[2]

How merciful our God is. He lets us connive and cheat to fulfill the vision of our pride, and then at the proper time, He confronts us and lets us see the true condition of our heart. It has well been said, "To be left alone with God is the only true way of arriving at a just knowledge of ourselves and our ways." Out of Jacob's confrontation came a name and a nature change. From here on he is known as Israel: *God ruled.* Jacob, who ruled with deceit and hypocrisy as he played the pantomime to become number one, became a God-ruled man. Perhaps there is hope for us too.

Endnotes:

1. James S. Hewett, *Illustrations Unlimited,* (Wheaton, Il.: Tyndale House Publishers, Inc., 1988).
2. Arthur W. Pink, *Gleaning in Genesis* (Grand Rapids: Kregel Publications, 1998).

Dear Jesus,

I am competitive by nature, and everything in me wants to be number one! Unfortunately, this often drives me to step on others, to disguise myself as being what I really am not, and it causes me to live a lie just to advance in my self-image. How this must grieve Your heart! Please forgive me. Help me to accept the role in life that You have assigned to me. Help me to know that You love me, even if I never rise to the top ten in life. Just being Your son should be enough for me.

Thank You.
Amen!

• • •

Questions

1. What promises has God personally given you? How have you striven to accomplish in your own strength (to make happen now) those things that God has promised instead of waiting for Him to fulfill His promises in His time?

2. In what areas do you need to trust God to fulfill His promises.

3. When have you experienced loss of the presence of God? How has discontent with His blessing effected your experience of His presence?

Chapter 7

PRIDE AND JEALOUSY

Miriam and Aaron began to talk against Moses because of his Cushite wife, for he had married a Cushite. "Has the LORD spoken only through Moses?" they asked. "Hasn't he also spoken through us?" And the LORD heard this.

(Now Moses was a very humble man, more humble than anyone else on the face of the earth.)

At once the LORD said to Moses, Aaron and Miriam, "Come out to the Tent of Meeting, all three of you." So the three of them came out. Then the LORD came down in a pillar of cloud; he stood at the entrance to the Tent and summoned Aaron and Miriam. When both of them stepped forward, he said, "Listen to my words:

> *"When a prophet of the LORD is among you,*
> *I reveal myself to him in visions,*
> *I speak to him in dreams.*
> *But this is not true of my servant Moses; he is faithful in all my house.*
> *With him I speak face to face, clearly and not in riddles; he sees the form of the LORD.*
> *Why then were you not afraid to speak against my servant Moses?"*

The anger of the LORD burned against them, and he left them. When the cloud lifted from above the Tent, there stood Miriam—leprous, like snow. Aaron turned toward her and saw that she had leprosy; and he said to Moses, "Please, my lord, do not hold against us the sin we have so foolishly committed. Do not let her be like a stillborn infant coming from its mother's womb with its flesh half eaten away."

So Moses cried out to the LORD, "O God, please heal her!"

The LORD replied to Moses, "If her father had spit in her face, would she not have been in disgrace for seven days? Confine her outside the camp for seven days; after that she can be brought back." So Miriam was confined outside the camp for seven days, and the people did not move on till she was brought back. Numbers 12:1-15, NIV

*P*ride does not always demand the number one position as it did in Jacob. Many times it will settle for equality in leadership, or even for control of leadership. Moses learned this the hard way as he led the released Hebrew slaves out of Egypt into the wilderness. Ten times, the people murmured against his leadership. They expressed dissatisfaction with the way, the water, the food, and His leadership in general. On one occasion, they voted Moses out of office and chose another leader who would return them to Egypt.

Every time the people revolted in dissatisfaction, God intervened with a plague that not only punished the dissenters, but it also got the attention of the rest of the people. God consistently reaffirmed His choice of Moses as the leader. Moses seemed to weather most of this discontentment, for he undoubtedly realized, as we now know, that criticism usually has its roots in proud jealousy.

In Numbers 12, we have the story of the ninth serious murmuring against Moses. This time it did not come from the mixed multitude; it came from the two leading personages in the congregation after Moses himself—Aaron and Miriam, Moses' own brother and sister. It would seem, from the silence of the Scriptures, that Aaron was duped into joining his sister in this revolt. He never demonstrated great strength of character in standing up to people, and he just couldn't tell his sister no. That God did not smite him with leprosy as He did Miriam strengthens my belief that Aaron was merely a weak support of Miriam's exploding pride.

Miriam had played a vital role in the life of Moses. When Moses' mother placed her baby boy in the Nile River in the crude ark made of bulrushes, it was Miriam who walked along the bank, keeping an eye on her baby brother. Watching Pharaoh's daughter take baby Moses out of the water and embrace him, it was Miriam who dared to approach the scene and offer to find a nursing mother from among the Hebrews to care for the baby. She obviously chose her own mother.

Eighty or so years later, when Moses returned to Egypt as the deliverer of the slaves, Miriam seemed to play a leading role with the women. Following the successful passage through the Red Sea and the subsequent destruction of Pharaoh's army, Miriam led the women in a tambourine dance as they joined in singing Moses' song: *"The horse and its rider he has hurled into the sea"* (Exodus 15:1, NIV). Miriam led the women in expressing praise to God, while Moses led the men in voicing their thanksgiving. It was a beautiful combination. Furthermore, Miriam prophesied with the full consent of Moses. He gladly gave her a place in Israel's spiritual leadership.

Now, however, Miriam, who had walked so very uprightly and righteously from her girlhood until the congregation of Israel stood at Mount Sinai, lost control of her pride and it exploded into jealousy.

It seems very likely that Miriam's outburst of hostility toward Moses surprised her as much as it surprised Moses. But such a level of pride can conceal itself behind a mask of humility and servanthood.

Another has commented, "Pride was in Miriam's heart; it must come out sooner or later. It was a pride that overwhelmed natural affection. It was a pride that made Miriam forget the obligations of her own honorable office. It was a pride that put on a pretense of being badly treated. It was, worst of all, spiritual pride. Pride of birth, of beauty, of wealth, of learning, all these are bad, often ridiculous; but spiritual pride is such a contradiction, such an amazing example of blindness, that we may well give it a preeminence among the evil fruits of the corrupt heart."[1]

Wounded Pride

The worst form of jealousy flows out of wounded pride, and once jealousy is released, there is no satiating it. It just will not be appeased. The more it is expressed, the bigger it becomes. The Bible says, *"Jealousy is cruel as the grave: the coals thereof are coals of fire, which hath a most vehement flame"* (Song of Solomon 8:6).

Pride consistently cringes when hearing another person praised, and the outworking of that wounded pride is often disastrous. The wise man wrote, *"Anger is cruel and fury overwhelming, but who can stand before jealousy?"* (Proverbs 27:4, NIV).

The dictionary defines *jealousy* as: "Hostility towards a rival or one believed to enjoy an advantage." This is what raged in Miriam. In her charge against Moses, we see prideful jealousy expressed three ways: first, against Moses' wife; second, against Moses' superior spiritual gift, and third, against the office that Moses held exclusively. This jealous explosion of pride brought serious accusations against God's ordained leadership.

The first focus of Miriam's pride was against the wife of Moses. The more Miriam nursed her wounded pride, the bolder she became in lashing out at Moses' wife. All wives of pastors know what this is like. Those who are dissatisfied with the pastor start by finding fault with his wife. Perhaps they fear a frontal attack against the pastor himself—just in case he is truly a man of God. Their dear wives are virtually defenseless, for no matter what they do, say, wear, or whether they minister publicly or not, it will be challenged as wrong. They can maintain their balance if they remember that they are not the primary target of such an attack.

Miriam followed this standard route of assault in attacking Moses' wife. During the time Moses dealt with Pharaoh in securing the release of the Hebrews, Zipporah, the wife of Moses, was nowhere to be found. She had returned to her father, while Moses was taking his family back to Egypt before his confrontation with the Pharaoh. Many commentators feel this separation occurred after the Lord demanded the circumcision of Moses' son. Zipporah was disgusted, and said, *"Surely a bloody husband art thou to me"* (Exodus 4:25). It is not unusual for our enemy to stir conflict in the home of one God has chosen to bring deliverance to others.

It is probable that Miriam, as the older sister, gave oversight to Moses' care during this time, as God was preparing to release the Hebrews from slavery. This sisterly care not only fed and clothed Moses; it also gave Miriam great prestige in the camp.

About the time God gave Moses the law on Mount Sinai, which you may remember was the area where Moses had tended his father-in-law's flock of sheep, Zipporah's father returned her to Moses. With the arrival of the wife of Moses (the powerful leader who had functioned until then as a single man in the congregation), Miriam found the respect she had enjoyed exclusively was then transferred to this stranger or divided with her, and this induced jealousy in Miriam.

It is not uncommon for some women in a congregation to be jealous of the pastor's wife, especially if the pastor marries after a season of serving the congregation as a single man. Miriam likely viewed Zipporah as competition for Moses' attention.

Religious Pride

Miriam's second outburst of jealous pride was directed at Moses' spiritual gift of hearing directly from God. It is possible that Miriam really was disturbed over Zipporah's return to Moses, but the odds are against it. Miriam was far less disturbed over Moses' newly-returned wife than she was upset over some new appointments Moses had made without consulting with Aaron and her. The great English commentator Matthew Henry said of this experience, "The pretense was that he had married a wife of foreign extraction; but probably the true reason was their pride was hurt, and their envy excited by his superior authority in the government of the people."[2] While this wife was the stated reason for Miriam's attack against Moses, only one sentence in this passage is given to it. The rest of the chapter is devoted to the other expressions of Miriam's jealousy.

We may find the real basis of this jealous outpouring of anger in the preceding chapter. God instructed Moses to appoint seventy elders. Then He took some of the anointing that rested on Moses and shared it with these other men. They immediately began to prophesy. Perhaps Miriam's pride was hurt because of having "competitors" in the prophetic ministry. As a prophetess, Miriam was distinguished above all the women of Israel, but the possession of great gifts does not necessarily involve the possession of great grace. A man or woman may hold high office in the church and yet sin grievously.

There is no evidence that Miriam ever wanted Moses' place, but she certainly desired the number two spot in the leadership. Now it appears that there are seventy others with the prophetic gift that Moses had brought into leadership. This great gift of spiritual insight and supernatural ability to communicate God's word and will had now been shared with many others.

This form of religious pride has been common in the church throughout history. Once the division between the clergy and laity was established, the clergy wanted to be known as the exclusive persons to hear God, understand His Word, and be able to communicate this to the people. Even Christ's disciples were disturbed when they heard of "nondisciples" preaching and working miracles. " *'Master,' said John, 'we saw a man driving out demons in your name and we tried to stop him, because he is not one of us."* *'Do not stop him,' Jesus said, 'for whoever is not against you is for you' "* (Luke 9:49-50, NIV). Even the disciples had this pride of exclusivity.

It was hard for Miriam, as it was for the disciples, to see others who had not "paid the price" flowing in the same gifts and ministries for which they had paid an extreme price. Similarly, some pastors cannot make room for the prophetic gifts to flow in the congregation.

Once the pride in Miriam had exploded into jealousy against Moses' wife and shared gift, the true reason for this outburst came to light. Her third attack came against the office that Moses held exclusively. Psychologists have long held that we all have three reasons for important actions, and more than likely it will be the third, and often hidden, reason that is the true motivator of the action. Miriam was jealous of the exclusive position, or office, her brother held. He had unilaterally appointed these elders without discussing it with her and Aaron.

The actual accusation this pair leveled against Moses was, *"Has the LORD spoken only through Moses? ... Hasn't he also spoken through us?"* (Numbers 12:1-2, NIV). Aaron and Miriam did hear from God—Miriam through the prophetic gift and Aaron through the Urim and Thummim, but Moses heard God speak to him directly—face-to-face.

Miriam made a mistake that is all too common today. She mistook gifts or anointing for office. Although God clearly told her that the way He spoke to Moses was far superior to the way He spoke to her, Miriam felt such an equality that she could suggest that Moses share his office with her. Perhaps she felt that the leadership should be in a family council—a forerunner of the church board. Having received a measure of the prophetic spirit, Miriam aspired to a share in the authority of Moses. She wanted to be part of the decision making for this new nation.

How devastating this could have been for Moses, to be forced to run everything God told Him to do through a committee—especially a family council. Just ask any pastor who works with a secular-minded church board.

My sister, Iverna Tompkins, with the help of her three brothers, conducted a monthly training class for ministers and church leaders for over a year. It was precious to see God's anointing transfer and rest upon both pastors and leaders. I was called into a pastor's study and quizzed about what was being taught and practiced in these sessions. He didn't seem very satisfied with my answer, so I pressed him for his reason in questioning me.

"Do you know a Mary Martha," [3] he asked?

"Yes," I said, "she attends our training classes quite regularly."

"Well, she is a member of my church, and she has worked in various departments with us. Last week she walked into my study, declaring that God had appointed her to be the associate pastor of this church. She further stated that you had trained her and ordained her to the ministry."

We had certainly sought to train her to be a faithful lay minister in the congregation, but we had never ordained her to be a pastor, nor had we tried to give her any form of office. Her pride had evidently elevated her sense of self-worth.

Is it possible that this same thing had happened to Miriam? Had pride in her prophetic ministry made her feel that she held equal office with Moses?

During the years of my traveling ministry, I was approached by a variety of persons who pointed out that they were as anointed as the pastor and probably even more capable in the pulpit. They wanted my support in removing the pastor and replacing him with them. My standard response was, "You may, indeed, be more talented and anointed, but you have not been appointed by God to be the pastor. Anointing does not produce office; appointment does."

Because of the close family relationship, Miriam may not have realized that her outburst of prideful jealousy caused her to make accusations against God's appointed leadership. This is serious to God. He accepts such accusations as directed against Himself.

In the Old Testament, God's standard judgment upon those who made accusations against His appointed leaders was leprosy. For example, look at the lives of Miriam, Gehazi, and Uzziah. It is more than likely that God's warning, *"Take heed in the plague of leprosy"* (Deuteronomy 24:8), was more than an admonition to diligently observe the laws about leprosy. It was a warning against making accusations against God's appointed leadership. The Jews called leprosy "the finger of God." It came first on a person's house, then on his clothing, and if he would not repent, on his physical body. When Miriam so blatantly challenged the leadership of Moses, God smote her with this dreaded disease. At the intercession of the tenderhearted Moses, God limited the duration of the disease in her to seven days. Who said there is no mercy in the Old Testament?

We can only wonder what went through Miriam's mind during those seven days she was separated from the camp. God often touches our bodies or natural circumstances to bring us face-to-face with our destructive pride. We do not see or hear of Miriam ever complaining against Moses again after God's severe judgment came upon her.

Endnotes:

1. Spence, H.D.M. and Excell, Joseph S., *The Pulpit Commentary*, Vol. II. (Grand Rapids, Mich.: William B. Eerdmans Publishing Co., 1962).
2. Matthew Henry, *Commentary on the Holy Bible*, , Vol. I. (Nashville: Thomas Nelson, Inc., 1979).
3. This is a fictitious name.

Dear Father,

You know, better than I, how prone I am to jealousy. When someone else gets the position I feel I deserve, my pride explodes within me and causes me to become jealous. I have learned to contain it, but it poisons my heart. Lord, sometimes I am even jealous when I see someone else get a special blessing from You. I know this is dirty, rotten pride and I detest it in myself. Please cleanse me of it. You have been so good to me; I have no reason to be jealous of anything You do for others.

Thank You for Your help.
Amen!

• • •

Questions

1. What is murmuring? Give an example from your own life.

2. Where are you vulnerable to jealousy? Is there any fear that goes with the jealousy?

3. Have you experienced others being jealous of your gift? How has God protected you?

4. With whom do you feel competitive? Experiment blessing others to do better and appear better than you do. *"Do nothing from selfish ambition or deceit, but in humility regard others better than yourselves"* (Philippians 2:3).

Chapter 8

PRIDE AND INSURRECTION

Now Korah ... along with Dathan and Abiram ... and On ... descendants of Reuben ... took two hundred and fifty Israelite men, leaders of the congregation, ... and they confronted Moses ... and ... Aaron, and said to them, "You have gone too far! All the congregation are holy, everyone of them, and the Lord is among them. So why then do you exalt yourselves above the assembly of the Lord?"

When Moses heard it, ... he said to Korah and his company, ... "The Lord will make known who is his, and who is holy, and who will be allowed to approach him. ... Do this: take censers, and tomorrow put fire in them, and lay incense on them before the Lord; and the man whom the Lord chooses shall be the holy one. You Levites have gone too far! Is it too little for you that the God of Israel has separated you from the congregation of Israel, to allow you to approach him in order to perform the duties of the Lord's tabernacle, and to stand before the congregation and serve them? ... Yet you seek the priesthood as well! Therefore you and all your company have gathered together against the Lord. What is Aaron that you rail against him?" ...

Moses said to Korah, "As for your and all your company, be present tomorrow before the Lord, ... and let each one of you take his censer, ... , two hundred fifty censers ... ."

Then Korah assembled the whole congregation against them ... . And the glory of the Lord appeared ... . The Lord spoke to Moses and to Aaron, saying, Separate yourselves from this congregation, so that I may consume them ... . They fell on their faces, and said, "O God, ... shall one person sin and you become angry with the whole congregation?"

And the Lord spoke to Moses, saying: Say to the congregation: "Get away from the dwellings of Korah, Dathan, and Abiram." ... Dathan and Abiram came out and stood at the entrance of their tents, together with their wives, their children, and their little ones. And Moses said, "This is how you shall know that the Lord has sent me to do these works; it has not been of my own accord: If these people die a natural death, ... then the Lord has not sent me. But if the ground opens its mouth and swallows them up, with all that belongs to them, ... then you shall know that these men have despised the Lord."

As soon as he finished speaking ... , the ground under them was split apart. The earth opened its mouth and swallowed them up, along with their households ... and all their goods ... and they perished. All Israel around them fled at their outcry. And fire came out from the Lord and consumed the two hundred fifty men offering the incense.   Numbers 16:1-35, NRS

*M*iriam's one week of banishment from Israel while suffering with leprosy may have seemed too light a punishment for such an outburst of jealous pride, but that really wasn't the end of it. We never again hear of her singing or leading the women in song, nor is there a biblical record of her ever prophesying again. Sometimes our choices in life have long-term consequences, even though God forgives our actions. Lusting for higher ministries sometimes costs us our place in lesser ministries. Instead of gaining more, we lose what we had. Just ask Korah.

But for God's grace, the humiliating and potentially deadly judgment of God upon Miriam's rebellion against Moses' leadership should have been a warning against all Israel. How unfortunate it is that few of us learn much from history—no matter how recent it may be.

For those who feel that Aaron got off without God's judgment, just read a few chapters more in the book of Numbers. Aaron did not escape judgment for his part in sharing with Miriam a complaint against Moses. God merely let him get a taste of insurrection from Korah and company. God sometimes punishes us directly, but often He lets other people do this work for Him. It is not at all unusual for God to allow others to do to us exactly what we have done to others.

This principle is illustrated in the book of Judges. King Adoni-bezek fled from a losing battle and, when captured, had his thumbs and big toes cut off. His response to this treatment was, *"Threescore and ten kings, having their thumbs and their great toes cut off, gathered their meat under my table: as I have done, so God hath requited me"* (Judges

1:7). Again, consider that the modern way of saying this is, "What goes around, comes around."

Aaron had repeatedly stood by Moses while people challenged his authority to lead, but now it was Aaron's turn to be challenged. The Levite priests Korah, Dathan, Abiram and On led a group of two hundred and fifty *"well-known community leaders who had been appointed members of the council"* (Numbers 16:2, NIV) in challenging Aaron's right to be Israel's high priest. The insurrection was based on a plea of "equality of the believers." They probably pointed out the obvious weaknesses in Aaron, while describing their own combined strengths. For all his failings, however, Aaron was God's appointed man for the office.

Korah, Dathan, and Abiram were among the priests of the Levitical tribe whom God had chosen to be assistants to the Aaronic priesthood. Without these priests, worship would have been impossible in Israel, for they were involved in all the Outer Court ministries—which included the offering of the sacrifices. The Levites were also keepers of the gates, the singers, and musicians who ministered before the Lord, and the persons God chose to move the wilderness Tabernacle and its furnishings from place to place. Only Aaron and his two sons held a place of higher respect and authority in the priesthood at this time.

The Levitical priests didn't live in the general encampment; they pitched their tents around the fence of the Tabernacle. They were considered holy persons in the camp.

Pride Is Ambitious

These three men learned what many others have since discovered— that it is difficult to be elevated in the eyes of others without pride becoming a dominant force in one's life. It is so comfortable to believe the good things others are saying about us. Unfortunately, pride does not stop at the praises of others. Pride is very ambitious. It suggests that it is absurd to remain number two when we might successfully become number one. It doesn't seem to matter to pride that someone else is already number one.

In their discontent with their lesser position in the priesthood, these men rebelled against Aaron. Pride had blinded their eyes to God's appointment, closed their minds to what had happened to Miriam for a lesser rebellion, and inflated their egos to the point of near explosion.

This scenario is played out in our churches on a regular basis. Staff members want to become the senior pastor, musicians want to become preachers, volunteer workers want to become paid staff members, while persons with a sense of self-importance engage in a power struggle to control both the pastor and the church. Pride, out-of-control pride, is behind all of this.

These three insurrectionists set a pattern for those who have followed them. They didn't challenge the leadership until they had polluted the congregation. We do not know how long it took these three men to convince these two hundred and fifty council members to join them in this rebellion, but finally the numbers seemed to be unbeatable—two hundred and fifty-three against two. There seemed to be no way these men could lose the contest. They had, however, failed to factor God into the equation.

When a takeover at any level is attempted, pride draws as many people into the conflict as possible. I have watched repeatedly as congregations have been divided, and sometimes destroyed, by the organized pride of one or two people set on having their own way. The cost in spiritual lives is seldom considered. Pride insists on having its own way—no matter the cost to others.

There are well-trained and consecrated ministers all across America who are working in the commercial world because someone let his or her pride organize a campaign against the pastor. Consequently, the pastor's effectiveness was destroyed, his self-image was diminished, and often his reputation was ruined—just so some layman could gain control of the church. Satan still has his Korahs whose pride can be stirred to become a destructive force.

Not all modern Korahs want the pastor's position; they just want to control him. When they fail, they leave the church, but they seldom leave alone. They launch a campaign of dissatisfaction and take as many church members with them as possible. They are so cowardly that they can't even leave alone. Just as these three rebels were the cause of the destruction of the two hundred and fifty men they had stirred up to join in the rebellion, so those who stir others to discontent often cause weak Christians to become discontented and disillusioned with the church and to fall away from Christ. What a terrible price for personal pride wanting its own way!

These men not only failed in their attempt to climb the ladder of success in the priesthood, but they paid the ultimate price—the loss of their lives. God instructed Moses to tell the men to stand at the opening of their tents with their wives, children, and possessions. Then the other Israelites were warned to separate themselves from them. Moses said that if these men were wrong in their challenge against the leadership of Aaron, the earth would open and swallow them.

The snickers of unbelief had hardly begun when the earth did open to devour Korah, Dathan, and Abiram, their families, and everything they owned. Then, while the people watched in disbelief, the two hundred and fifty council members were consumed by a fire sent from Heaven.

This must have weakened the government of Israel for a season, for that is a very large number of key leaders to lose in a day. Pastor friends of mine can relate to this, for they have had key leadership walk off to join or start another church. These pastors had spent years training those leaders, but they chose to rise up against their teachers, and when they could not prevail, they walked away—leaving the local congregation without qualified leadership.

Does God judge such actions today? Oh, yes! Perhaps not as dramatically as in Moses' time, but very decidedly. Men who commit such acts may go through the motions of being alive, but they are often already spiritually dead. They may build a religious organization, but it will be without the life and the presence of God. It is rare for a church born from a split to ever amount to anything. The pride that brought it into being will eat away at it like a cancer until it ultimately destroys itself.

The story we are looking at has an even darker side to it. The morning after the three Levites were entombed in the earth and God's fire consumed the two hundred and fifty men who had joined in the revolt, the remainder of the congregation came to Moses and Aaron and accused them of being responsible for these deaths. This so angered God that He sent a plague among the people, while threatening to destroy the entire nation. Moses sent Aaron into the congregation with a censer (incense burner) and incense to appease the wrath of God. God let this display of worship (which is what incense speaks of) quench His anger, but not until fourteen thousand seven hundred Israelites had been killed.

Pride Is Infectious

Why did this happen? The insidious pride of these three Levites became so infectious that not only did two hundred and fifty elders join their scheme to replace Aaron, but the *"entire congregation"* took their side when God punished them. This gives us some indication of how widely the vocal campaign had spread in the camp before the uprising became a fact.

Many apparently fail to realize just how far their criticism of their leaders reaches. In order to get our "two hundred and fifty council members" to stand with us, we pollute hundreds, even thousands, more. We may speak to one or two persons, but they speak to a few others, who share it with their friends, who share it with their e-mail list, until it is finally placed on a website for all of the world to read. Wouldn't it be wonderful if the true Gospel could spread that rapidly?

Why is this story recorded in the Bible? Paul told us, *"Now these things occurred as examples to keep us from setting our hearts on evil things as they did. ... These things happened to them as examples and were written down as warnings for us, on whom the fulfillment of the ages has come"* (1 Corinthians 10:6 and 11, NIV).

Attempting to overthrow God's appointed leadership is not only dangerous. It can be deadly. God protects the man or woman He calls into the ministry. He is jealous over His Church.

I am not suggesting that we should blindly follow our church leaders. They can sometimes be wrong like anyone else, but there are channels we should go through to bring correction. I wouldn't want to be a part of any church that did not have a stated routine of discipline for its leaders as well as for its followers.

This is a far cry from the organized campaigns to throw the pastor out of office and out of town. What if he or she is really God-appointed to your congregation? You will find yourself fighting against God, and either way the issue goes, you will lose.

Rereading this passage in Numbers will make it clear that Korah, Dathan, Abiram and On had no complaint about the actual leadership of Moses or Aaron. There were no charges against their moral behavior or their spiritual sensitivity. The only problem was the exclusivity of the positions and the pride of these men in wanting to share in the glory of leadership at the top. They had set themselves to become equal to Aaron—no matter what it might cost. Like Miriam, they lost! And so will you if you join in an insurrection against your pastor.

Dear Jesus,

It is embarrassing to admit to You how often I have felt that I was more capable than some of the leaders You have placed over me. Sometimes they seem so inept or lazy that I want to step in, replace them, and show others how it should be done. No, that isn't really honest. Please forgive my spirit of insurrection. If You wanted me in that office, You would have put me in it. Please don't let my inner discontent bring me to the point of seeking to discipline or unseat Your servants. I humble myself before You to work with whomever You appoint.

Thank You.
Amen!

• • •

Questions

1. Summarize the teaching of this chapter in your own words.

2. What helps you support others in leadership and not fight against them?

3. What are some of the woundings you or your church have experienced caused by insurrection? Share them with someone who can pray with you for healing.

4. How do you identify with Moses and Aaron?

Chapter 9

PRIDE AND MINISTRY

And Balak ... saw all that Israel had done to the Amorites. And Moab was ... afraid ... . He sent messengers unto Balaam ..., saying, ... Come ..., curse ... this people ... . And the elders of Moab and ... Midian departed with the rewards of divination ...; and they came unto Balaam, and spake ... the words of Balak. ... And God said unto Balaam, Thou shall not go with them; thou shalt not curse the people: for they are blessed. ... And the princes ... went unto Balak, and said, Balaam refuseth to come with us.

And Balak sent ... more honourable than they. And they ... said, ... Let nothing ... hinder thee from coming ... : for I will promote thee unto very great honour: ... come therefore ..., curse me this people. ... And God ... said unto him, ... Rise up, and go with them; but yet the word which I ... say, ... that shalt thou do. ...

And ... on the morrow, ... Balak took Balaam ... up into the high places ... that ... he might see ... the people.

Numbers 22:2-41

And Balaam said ..., Build me ... seven altars, and prepare ... seven oxen and seven rams. And Balak and Balaam offered on every altar a bullock and a ram. ... And God met Balaam ... and ... put a word in Balaam's mouth... .

And the LORD met Balaam ... and said, Go again unto Balak, and say ...: God is not a man, that he should lie; neither the son of man, that he should repent ... . Behold, I have received commandment to bless ... and I cannot reverse it.

Numbers 23:1-20

And when Balaam saw that it pleased the LORD to bless Israel, he went not ... to seek for enchantments, but he set his face toward the wilderness. And ... he saw Israel ...; and the spirit of God came upon him. ...

And Balak's anger was kindled against Balaam, and he ... said ..., I called thee to curse mine enemies, and ... thou hast ... blessed them ... three times. Therefore now flee ... to thy place: I thought to promote thee ...; but ... the LORD ... kept thee back from honour. Numbers 24:1-11

*K*orah and company illustrate a proud attempt to control by declaring an equality with leadership, but Balaam pictures an attempt to destroy both the leadership and its followers with spiritual curses.

Balaam is both a mystery and a conundrum to Bible students. Some just pass the story off as folklore, especially since much of it is poetic in form. Still, the Bible devotes three chapters to this story, and Balaam's name is mentioned about fifty times in these chapters and an additional ten times in other passages, including three times in the New Testament. It seems far wiser to accept the story as actual, factual, and illustrative. To discount Balaam as merely a false prophet is to miss the true point of the story. He was far less a false prophet than he was an extremely proud prophet.

Archaeologists say that Balaam's name was written on wall plaster at Tel Deir Alle in the Jordan valley about 700 B.C. This text reveals the seer's wider fame. Apparently, Balaam was not the only person who thought he was the great one.

Balaam's story begins in Numbers 22, where the children of Israel have pitched their tents in the plains of Moab. Balak, the king of Moab, was fearful of Israel, for he was fully aware of what they had done to the Amorites. Rather than meet them with armed strength, he chose to use spiritual incantations to destroy them. He sent elders with the rewards of divination in their hands to convince Balaam to come and curse Israel. Balak's message was simply *"Now come and put a curse on these people, because they are too powerful for me. ... For I know that those you bless are blessed, and those you curse are cursed"* (Numbers 22:6, NIV).

Being sought out by the king of the land surely stirred Balaam's pride, and the price being offered for his services proved to Balaam that he was finally coming into his own. He may well have felt, "Have gift; will travel." The price seemed right to Balaam, but he asked for the night to inquire of God. God said, "No!" so Balaam remained at home.

A second and more honorable group of officials came later with a far bigger bribe, and Balaam convinced God to let him go with them. We remember the angelic confrontation on the route to Moab and the speaking donkey, but Balaam pressed on. Three times, on three separate mountains, he offered sacrifices and sought a word from God. Each time God blessed Israel and prevented Balaam from cursing the people. In anger, Balak sent Balaam home without a reward.

Balaam Knew God's Voice

My strongest argument against calling Balaam a false prophet is that he could actually converse with God. Although he was not an Israelite, and, as far as we know, he had no contact with any of Israel's prophets, Balaam had learned how to contact God and communicate with Him. This underscores Peter's point, when he said, *"I now realize how true it is that God does not show favoritism but accepts men from every nation who fear him and do what is right"* (Acts 10:34-35, NIV). God has always loved Israel, but He has also made Himself available to the "whosoevers" of the world.

Both times when emissaries came to Balaam, pleading with him to come to Balak and curse Israel, Balaam talked with God about it. There is no evidence of witchcraft or incantation. He seems to have simply gone to his room and had a talk with Jehovah. Furthermore, Balaam was alert to the spirit world, for he showed no amazement at the appearance of an angel who talked with him, or even when an angel's voice came from his donkey.

In the manner of a true prophet, Balaam could receive a message from God and deliver it accurately to people. His statements about Israel and her future are pure words from the heart of God. Like all true prophets, Balaam could talk to God, hear from Him, see into the spirit world, and faithfully declare the words of God. How we could wish that many of the persons who call themselves prophets today had these same capacities!

Balaam's problem was not that he was false, but that he was mixed. He could contact God, and, apparently, also contact the demonic realm, for God is not in the business of cursing or carrying out curses. Balaam had a reputation for successfully bringing spiritual curses on others, and that's a form of witchcraft.

The most dangerous prophet in the world is one who is a mixture. He or she may accurately hear from God and share divine words with us—thereby producing in us a strong confidence. About that time, he or she shifts into another spirit realm and declares lies, condemnation, and false doctrine. Because we have heard truth from them, we often fail to judge the message by God's Word and discern the spirit force that is at work in the individual speaking. I believe Balaam falls into this category. Sometimes he spoke for God, but at other times he spoke for demonic forces. Probably there were times when he spoke just for Balaam.

Balaam Knew God's Will

Even a cursory reading of this passage in Numbers makes it clear that Balaam knew the will of God in this matter of going to Balak. God clearly said, "No!" As another has said, "He is not content to know God's will, but tries by every means in his power to cajole God into changing His mind, or, in other words, making wrong right. Five times he attempts to obtain God's consent, and always fails."

It sounds familiar, doesn't it? We claim we want to know the will of God, but in fact we want God to approve our will. If you doubt this, I dare you to record some of your prayer time and play it back a few days later. You will find yourself giving God orders and making your case like a clever lawyer. We want what we want when we want it far more than we want to know and do the will of God. It is sadly true that the curse of pride is that it still lifts our will and way above the will and way of God.

Jesus said, *"If ye know these things, happy are ye if ye do them"* (John 13:17). It doesn't impress God very much for us to finally know what He wants. He seeks obedient action.

Balaam Tried to Merchandise God

More than a hundred years ago, Dr. James Hastings wrote, "Balaam's persistence is evidently due to selfishness and greed."[1] Balaam learned what many current Christians know—that any spiritual gift from God is saleable—God's gifts can be used as merchandise. Most people are unwilling to pay the price to come into God's presence, but they are willing to pay almost any asking price to receive ministry from one who has come into that presence.

Pastors have told me that some persons with a ministry of healing, prophecy, or words of wisdom and knowledge are asking an advance fee of thousands of dollars for a single service in a local church. A pastor friend of mine told me that the speaker he had scheduled for a women's rally had to cancel because of sickness just two days before the scheduled meeting. He phoned a well-known gospel singer and comedian to see if she might be able to fill this slot. The response was, "Yes, I can come, but my fee is four thousand dollars for a forty-five-minute program." Understandably, the pastor became the speaker for the meeting. The "entertainment fee" was far too high for his budget.

This is even more pronounced in some of our more popular gospel musicians. They may call this ministry, but I believe God would call it merchandising a divine gift. How naive Jesus must have been when He told His disciples—and us, *"Heal the sick, cleanse the lepers, raise the dead, cast out devils: freely ye have received, freely give"* (Matthew 10:8).

If God put a dollar sign on His gifts to us, few, if any, of us would be saved, healed, blessed, or assured of a place in Heaven. What extreme pride, then, for us to feel that we have a right to demand a specified fee before ministering what God has entrusted to us.

Pride and Ministry

I understand Paul's practical teaching that, *"The Lord has commanded that those who preach the gospel should receive their living from the gospel"* (1 Corinthians 9:14, NIV). There is a vast difference between receiving whatever offering may be made available and setting fees or gouging an audience.

You may have seen it in conferences or on Christian television—proud ministers promising to impart some of the same anointing in which they minister to anyone who gives a specified amount of money. God is not for sale! The heart of the Gospel is, *"God so loved the world, that he gave"* (John 3:16). It appears that a spirit of greed and selfishness has replaced the spirit of giving that motivated our early pioneers in the faith. Balaam is a classic example of this greed.

How could any of us become so proud as to feel we have a right to sell God? I once heard a missionary tell how he was trying to do translation work in a particular tribe and found it hard to translate the word *pride,* or at least the concept. He finally came to the idea to use their word or words for the ears being too far apart. In other words, he conveyed the idea of an "inflated head," which is probably hard to improve on when we talk of the problem of pride. Enough said!

Balaam felt he was worth every dollar that was offered to him. He tried three times to deliver the requested curses, but each time God overruled him and pronounced wonderful blessings on the children of Israel. Balaam's ministry seems to have come to a crashing end. God may gift a person, but He does not have to put up with continued exploitation of that gift. Just a glance backward will reveal dozens of yesterday's "shooting stars" crushed and out of the ministry. These words are still in the Bible: *"Be not deceived; God is not mocked: for whatsoever a man soweth, that shall he also reap"* (Galatians 6:7). When we merchandise the gifts of God, Jehovah often cuts off the supply of the gifts and leaves us spiritually bankrupt.

Balaam Didn't Live a Godly Life

Like that of far too many visible and powerful ministers today, Balaam's character was far below his *charismata*—his gifts from God.

More and more we hear of powerful ministers declaring themselves to be exceptions to God's commands. Their morality is suspect, their marriages disintegrate and they trade marriage partners, while their handling of money is often downright shameful. Such people sometimes live just like the world lives, while declaring the glorious truths of Heaven. They live private lives that would have discounted their ministry in a previous, less polluted generation.

Balaam stated his desire to die the death of the righteous, but he was unwilling to live the life of the righteous. *"Who can count the dust of Jacob, and the number of the fourth part of Israel? Let me die the death of the righteous, and let my last end be like his!"* (Numbers 23:10).

The International Standard Bible Encyclopedia comments, "Though an element of mystery surrounds Balaam in the Old Testament narratives, the Scriptures leave us in no doubt as to what conclusions to draw with regard to his character. He is represented as the archetype of the false teachers of the Christian Church who pervert the truth of the Gospel in the interests of personal gain (see 2 Peter 2:15) and under the guise of Christian liberty advocate compromise with the world (see Revelation 2:14)."[2]

Character is all-important to God. He is in the process of making us *"be conformed to the likeness of his Son, that he might be the firstborn among many brothers"* (Romans 8:29, NIV). What we *are* has always been more important to God than what we *do.*

God is not using us as slave labor on the earth. He is preparing us for Heaven, and our ministry is part of that preparation. God is not nearly as interested in teaching us to heal the sick and deliver persons from drug addiction as He is in making us holy men and women through whom He can save the lost, heal the sick, and work miracles in the lives of believers.

The greatest hindrance to the display of God's mighty power in and through His ministers, which includes all believers, is lack of character in the channels available to Him. God knows that unless a Christ-like character has been formed in us, a display of divine power through us will probably produce inordinate pride that might destroy us. Isn't this what Peter had in mind when, under the inspiration of the Spirit of God, he wrote: *"All of you, clothe yourselves with humility toward one another, because, 'God opposes the proud but gives grace to the humble' "* (1 Peter 5:5, NIV).

As J.I. Packer says, "The focus of health in the soul is humility, while the root of inward corruption is pride. In the spiritual life, nothing stands still. If we are not constantly growing downward into humility, we shall be steadily swelling up and running to seed under the influence of pride."[3] This is what happened to Balaam. It will happen to us as well if we continue to minister with a swollen-head feeling of great worth. Remove the work of the cross from our lives, and none of us is worth the price of a hamburger at Burger King.

There has to be a reason for three complete chapters being devoted to Balaam. The New Testament gives us a clue, for Peter warns, *"They have left the straight way and wandered off to follow the way of Balaam son of Beor, who loved the wages of wickedness"* (2 Peter 2:15, NIV). Jude says, *"Woe unto them! for they have gone in the way of Cain, and ran greedily after the error of Balaam for reward, and perished in the gainsaying of Core"* (Jude 11).

Whether we are pastors or "pew warmers," we need to constantly guard our pride levels—lest, in one way or another, we put a price on our service to the people of God. This will quickly make false prophets of us.

Endnotes:

1. James Hastings, M.A., D.D., *A Dictionary of the Bible* (New York: Charles Scribner's Sons, 1858).
2. *The International Standard Bible Encyclopedia*, Vol. I (Grand Rapids, Mich.: William B. Eerdmans Publishing Co., 1979).
3. J.I. Packer, *Rediscovering Holiness*, in *Christianity Today*, Vol. XXXVI, No. 13.

Dear Lord,

You have been so kind to share some of Your gifts and spiritual ministries with me. What a blessing they are both to me and to others! Lately, I have seen how others have learned to merchandise these gifts, and they seem to be living very well. I sometimes wonder if I should do the same. If people are willing to pay for it, why shouldn't I charge for my services? O, Lord, I know this is wrong. Please forgive my greed. You freely gave me these gifts—expecting me to share them freely with others. Please keep my motives pure so that I can minister out of a clean heart.

Thank You.
Amen!

• • •

Questions

1. God would not allow Balaam to curse, only bless. Do an experiment. Intercede for someone, declaring that only words of blessing will come upon him or her, even though others want to curse them.

2. Have you known anyone who prophesied a mixture of truth from God along with words that were false? How did you discern the difference? What helped?

3. Summarize the teaching of this chapter in your own words.

Chapter 10

PRIDE AND PRESUMPTION

Now the children of Reuben and ... Gad had a ... multitude of cattle: and when they saw the land of Jazer and ... Gilead ... was a place for cattle; the children of Gad and ... Reuben came and spake unto Moses, and to Eleazar ..., saying, ... If we have found grace in thy sight, let this land be given unto thy servants for a possession, and bring us not over Jordan.

And Moses said ..., Shall your brethren go to war, and shall ye sit here? And ... discourage ye the heart of the children of Israel from going over into the land which the LORD hath given them? ...

And they ... said, We will build sheepfolds here for our cattle, and cities for our little ones: but we ... will go ... before the children of Israel, until we have brought them unto their place ... . We will not return ... until the children of Israel have inherited every man his inheritance. ...

And Moses said ..., If ye will do this thing, ... this land shall be your possession before the LORD. ... Build you cities ..., and folds for your sheep; and do that which hath proceeded out of your mouth. ... And the children of Gad and ... Reuben answered, saying, ... We will pass over ... into ... Canaan, that ... this side [of] Jordan may be ours. And Moses gave unto them ... the kingdom ... of the Amorites, and ... Bashan.

Numbers 32:1-33

*I*t was the season for change. Israel's winter of wandering was about to give place to the spring of entering the Promised Land. Preparations were being made, and speculation was rampant throughout the camp. Perhaps the people most disturbed about the move were the members of the tribes of Gad and Reuben, who felt that they had too much to lose by entering this new land. The more they talked about it, the stronger they felt, and half the tribe of Manasseh joined them in protesting having to cross over.

This was not rebellion, as their fathers had dissented after hearing the negative report of the ten spies some forty years earlier. Neither was this hysteria, or fear, of facing conflict, for they had volunteered to join in the fight of conquest, providing they did not have to live in the land once it was conquered.

No, they were not against the others conquering the territory; they simply did not want to give up what they already possessed. They proudly presumed that nothing on the other side of the Jordan could equal what they already possessed on the east side of the river.

Pride in Prosperity Hinders Progress

These two and a half tribes had done exceedingly well with the flocks and herds they had inherited from their fathers. By all the standards of that time, they were prosperous—very prosperous. It was observed as far back as 458 B.C., "Those who prosper take on airs of vanity."[1] This seems to have been the case with these particular tribes, for they approached Moses with a request (probably more of a legal brief) to give them the territory they now occupied as their inheritance. Their argument, in essence, was, "We're too rich to move with you." After some qualifications were added to the petition, Moses granted their desires.

Whether they realized it or not, they were cutting themselves off from God's provisions, promises, and presence. They would be far removed from the Tabernacle and its priestly ministries, and they would be separated from Israel's government. They proudly presumed that they would be able to take care of these needs themselves. Had they forgotten that everything they possessed had come as a gift from God's hand?

These tribes also failed to realize that what God had given to them was merely an *"earnest of [their] inheritance"* (Ephesians 1:14). There was far more waiting for them across the river than they had already received. Settling for God's past blessings will always hinder our pressing into the fullness of God's inheritance for our lives.

This was illustrated by Christ's confrontation with the young ruler who came asking how to inherit eternal life. When he affirmed that he had kept all the commandments, Jesus said that he lacked one thing. He should sell what he had and give to the poor. When the rich ruler said that he couldn't do that because he was very rich, *"Jesus looked at him and said, 'How hard it is for the rich to enter the kingdom of God!' "* (Luke 18:24, NIV).

There is nothing wrong with having an abundance...unless we allow our possessions to possess us. How sad to let an abundance, both spiritually and naturally, keep us from walking further into the provisions and promises of God!

Far too often, prosperity replaces the sense of a need for God. Just before the people of Israel entered into the Promised Land, God reminded them that He was giving them houses they had not built, vineyards they had not planted, and wells they had not dug. He warned them not to forsake Him in the midst of this prosperity (see Deuteronomy 6). Later, by the voice of the prophet, God laments that when He blessed Israel, they turned from Him, but when He sold them into slavery, they sought His face. It seems that they really didn't want *Him;* they just wanted His gifts.

We see this same principle at work in America today. When we struggled financially, we sought the face of God, but now that we are at a high level of prosperity, God has been removed from our schools, our thoughts, and all our lives. With prosperity, there usually comes a high level of pride. Perhaps as long as we feel we are able to do for ourselves, we do not depend on God.

Pastors have long complained that people come to church when in need, but they forsake the church once the need has been met. Many Christians seem less interested in progressing in God than in prospering in life. They include God in their lives for what they can get from Him. At all other times, they prefer to stay "on the other side of the Jordan." They really do not want to live close to God, for He might interfere with their lifestyles. "I can do it myself" is the cry of their proud hearts.

Pride of Possessions Anchors Us in the Past

These two and a half tribes had never known the whip of a slave master, nor had they experienced the great deliverance from Egypt. They were the second generation of Hebrews in the wilderness. The first generation had already died off there. The large flocks of sheep and herds of cattle that stirred such pride in them had originally been brought out of Egypt by their parents. They had been great caretakers of the things their fathers had left to them. Now, rather than go into the Promised Land and capture new territory to be passed on to their own children, they contented themselves with being caretakers of past blessings.

Is this a picture of the major religious denominations of today? Several generations ago, God brought their forefathers into new spiritual liberty and truth. This truth was clothed in doctrine, housed in church structures, and protected by a religious political system. To insure the preservation of this truth, universities and seminaries were birthed so that it could be correctly taught to children and grandchildren. Succeeding generations not only protected this truth, but greatly enlarged it.

Each denomination has sheltered what it received from God as though God would never again give anything new. When God did come on the scene again and offer a fresh revelation of Himself, like these two and a half tribes, the people of many existing denominations preferred to remain in the old revelation rather than enter into the new. As a matter of fact, Christian historians affirm that those who have experienced a prior move of God have often become persecutors of a new move of God. They not only do not want to go in themselves, they don't even care to believe that something greater is being offered.

Moving into new truth and experience appears to be threatening to many existing church leaders because it brings with it the fear of losing control. Anything new is threatening to most people, but it is especially intimidating to leadership. It seems safer to remain in the old than to accept the challenge of the new. Their houses and barns have been built on the far side of the Jordan, and they are content to spend the rest of their lives there.

This same failure can be seen in individual churches. Far too many pastors in America are merely caretakers, and their people want it that way. It seems safer to remain in the past than to trust God and walk with Him into the future. They have found a beautiful oasis in the wilderness, and they intend to live the rest of their lives there, even if it dooms their children to remain forever in the wilderness while others move on into greater promises and provisions. What they now possess is minuscule compared to what God has available for them. *"However, as it is written: 'No eye has seen, no ear has heard, no mind has conceived what God has prepared for those who love him' "* (1 Corinthians 2:9, NIV).

Pride in Heritage Prevents Enlargement

When I was a pastor in a major denomination, I was filled with denominational pride. After all, we were the greatest, weren't we? I knew that God had revealed to us a wonderful spiritual truth that many other Christians had ignored or rejected. My father and grandfather had proclaimed this truth in that same denominational setting. I felt that what was good enough for them was good enough for me. I had inherited much from them.

In my pride, I was totally closed to any new revelation, although I did not know it and would have argued with you if you had told me. I was prepared to remain the rest of my life on the other side of the Jordan, for I thought this was all God had for my generation. Mercifully, God opened my spiritual eyes and let me see that there was, indeed, something more being offered to the Church in my time. I dared to believe that God's provision on the other side of the Jordan was better than what I was experiencing at the time. God's promises were available, but I had to go to them. They would be fulfilled only in the Promised Land, not on the other side of the Jordan.

What I have said about denominations and churches is equally true of individual believers. Many Christians do not want to move out of their comfort zones. Having found satisfaction in their salvation, it seems threatening to move into a life of sanctification or to live the Spirit-filled life. This divine redemption has made them rich compared to the life they used to live, so they lack the necessary motivation to press on into the greater things God has provided for all of us. Too many believers are content to remain on the *"east side of the Jordan."*

The land these tribes wanted to inherit had been captured in victorious battles against Sihon, king of the Amorites, and Og, king of Bashan. It is likely that these were training battles for the Hebrews who had to learn warfare, but neither of these two nations was among the seven nations God had planned for Israel to defeat.

How easy it is to be content with a training victory instead of preparing for the real conflict that lies ahead. Every victory that God gives us is great, but none of them are conclusive. The war isn't over yet.

I believe God intends to take this present generation into new territory, but that territory is occupied. While we have been relaxing in the spoils of past victories, the enemy has taken over our school systems, our entertainment industry, the moral fiber of our nation, and the minds of thousands of men and women through drugs and pornography. Dare we sit comfortably on the east side of the Jordan resting on the laurels of past victories and living in the luxury that our fathers have provided, and refuse to go in and possess the land that God wants to give us?

I grant you that these tribes kept their word and joined in the successful conquest under Joshua, but then they returned to the east side of the Jordan to live. The problem Israel faced is that they lacked enough men and women to inhabit the land they conquered. It is one thing to defeat an enemy, but still another thing to possess his territory. Israel's subsequent problems with the Canaanites, and with the six other "ites," was that after conquering their territory, they couldn't possess it. The loss of these two and a half tribes amplified that problem.

This is characteristic of most moves of God. Revivals draw far more people who will look, listen, and learn than people who are willing to move into the new territory and live there. We conquer territory that the devil quickly regains simply by moving back into uninhabited areas. In the meantime, Christians live in past blessings and seem unconcerned about today's generation.

If we do not move on into the new, our current riches will become antiques, at best. The first new automobile my father was able to purchase was a 1941 Plymouth sedan. At the time, it was an automobile with the most modern features. He and the entire family were understandably proud of it. However, it wouldn't be the car you would want to drive around today. A 1941 sedan would be so technologically outdated that only a lover of antique cars would want to own it or drive it.

Similarly, our spiritual riches of today will be outdated tomorrow. We need to move into new territory as God leads us on. We must be prepared to conquer the territory God leads us into. If we do not, we, like these two and a half tribes, will find ourselves cut off from what God is doing currently. Maybe we need to heed God's cry through the prophet Micah, *"Get up, go away! For this is not your resting place, because it is defiled, it is ruined, beyond all remedy"* (Micah 2:10, NIV). It may not look defiled to us now because we are comparing it to the wilderness, but wait until you see what is in the Promised Land of God's provision. When we see it, where we now live in pride will seem like the city slums by comparison.

Endnote:

1. *Agamemnon* (458 B.C.) trans. Richmond Lattimore

Dear Heavenly Father,

I am thankful for all the blessings, both physical and spiritual, You have poured out on my life and home. It is so much more than I deserve. Unfortunately, You and I both know how comfortable I have become living in this level of Your provision. Please forgive me, for I now realize that this is hindering my progression into the greater things You have prepared for me. Lord, I admit that I hold tightly to the past for the security it offers me. Please increase my trust in You and my faith in Your promises, so I can let go of my grip on the past and reach out to the glorious future You have prepared for me.

I really didn't realize the level of pride that caused me to grasp my present so tightly that it was costing me my future. I humble myself before You and acknowledge that without You, I am nothing and have nothing. I can't see what You see, but I can see You with the eyes of faith. Please lead me on, even if You have to drag me to get me started.

In Jesus' name,
Amen!

• • •

Questions

1. What is your *"eastside of the Jordan"* that you have difficulty letting go of? Is pride the reason for this?

2. What new revelations have you received from God in the last five years? What new movements of the Spirit are you embracing?

3. What helps you possess the land of your spiritual inheritance (for example, being desperate for a fresh experience of God's power and presence)?

Chapter 11

PRIDE AND POSITION

*And when the inhabitants of Gibeon heard what Joshua had done unto Jericho and to Ai, they ... made as if they had been ambassadors, and took old sacks upon their asses ... and old shoes ... and old garments ... and all the bread ... was dry and mouldy. And they went to ... Joshua ... and said ..., We be come from a far country: now ... make ye a league with us. And the men of Israel said ..., How shall we make a league with you? And they said ..., We are thy servants. And Joshua said ..., Who are ye? and from whence come ye? And they said unto him, From a very far country thy servants are come because of ... the L*ORD *... : for we have heard ... all that he did in Egypt, and all that he did to the two kings of the Amorites ... . Wherefore our elders ... spake to us, saying, ... Go to meet them, and say unto them, ... Make ye a league with us. ... And the men ... asked not counsel at the mouth of the L*ORD*. And Joshua made peace with them, and made a league with them, to let them live ... . And ... at the end of three days ..., they heard that they were their neighbours, and that they dwelt among them. ... And all the congregation murmured against the princes. But all the princes said unto all the congregation, We have sworn unto them by the L*ORD *God of Israel: now therefore we may not touch them.* Joshua 9:3-19

*F*rom the time of our birth, we have a position in life. Usually a baby is number one in the home and seems to be in total control of the household. One good cry and the parents come running. As we mature, our position changes in relationship to the other members of the household. If there are siblings, there will be a constant vying for a higher position of authority among them.

The more we mature in life, the more we see our positions enlarging and changing. In school, we may be the captain of a sports team or the leader in an academic study. When we marry, we take on a whole new role. The coming of children gives us more positional authority than we have ever experienced. The job we take for earning an income may also offer us further positions of authority.

It is automatic for us to take pride in our position. Think of how a young lady flashes her engagement ring around for everyone to see. She is proud of her coming marriage to Mr. Right. She is about to take on the position of his wife, and, hopefully, then become the mother of his children. Although few women think of it at the time, she will eventually fill the position of grandmother in the years ahead. She will live her life in the pride of these positions, and she will exercise the authority that comes with these roles. In today's world, she may also hold down a job that has to be juggled with her position at home.

What is true of us individually is equally true of us collectively. There cannot be civilization without leadership, and this calls for some to occupy the position of leaders. In Moses' time, these leaders were called princes. They ruled with Moses and, later, with Joshua.

Leadership carries great responsibilities with it. These princes, whom Moses had trained, knew their own people quite well, but they faced an entirely different type of people as they entered into the Promised Land. Israel's princes had dealt exclusively with covenant people, to whom truth was an imperative in life. They were ill-prepared to deal with deceit and dishonesty. It is usually the honest person who is the most susceptible to deception, for he expects others to think and behave as he does.

The people of Israel had hardly finished celebrating their unprecedented victory over Jericho and Ai when some men, pretending to be ambassadors from a far country, approached the elders in rags, with moldy bread and empty drinking vessels. They claimed that they had come from a distant country and wanted to plead for peace. God had provided for this in Deuteronomy 20:16, but this applied only to persons living outside the Promised Land.

Positional Authority Often Leads to Pride

Being petitioned for peace was a totally new experience for both Joshua and the princes. No king had ever surrendered to Moses or Joshua. The princes of Israel were accustomed to confrontation, and conciliation was a whole new experience for them. It must have stirred great pride in them to have these ambassadors bow before them and plead for mercy. It made "big men" of them.

It was probably this extreme pride that kept Joshua and the princes from more closely examining the fake ambassadors and seeking God for His input. They were totally taken in by the deceit. These men were good actors; and why not? Their very lives depended on making this ruse believable.

God, through Moses, instructed the princes in the way to deal with each individual nation. Deuteronomy 20 is very detailed. It seems that the pride in their position caused these princes to make judgments on circumstantial evidence instead of asking God for the facts as He saw them.

Jesus taught us that our enemy is a deceiver and a liar, and John even affirmed that *"the truth is not in him"* (1 John 2:4). Whenever we deal with Satan's kingdom, we are at a disadvantage, for he plays very loose with the truth. He sometimes makes black look like white. In any business concerns with him, we need the legal counsel of one who knows him and his ways. And no one knows him better than his Creator, Jesus Christ.

The psalmist said, *"Blessed is the nation whose God is the LORD,"* and, *"Yea, happy is that people, whose God is the LORD"* (Psalms 33:12 and 144:15). What wisdom is available to such a nation! Israel had received wisdom, the Law, and the commandments from her God. But God is not honor-bound to impart His wisdom to a nation's leaders unless they ask for it. Israel's rulers felt that they were capable of making this decision on their own, and God did not thunder His disapproval from Heaven. Neither will He do so for America. If we ask, God will guide us, but merely having "IN GOD WE TRUST" on our money does not mean that our princes will make right decisions. God spoke through Jeremiah, telling us, *"Call unto me, and I will answer thee, and show thee great and mighty things, which thou knowest not"* (Jeremiah 33:3).

These princes not only decided without consulting with God; they also swore to the Gibeonites in the name of God. A few days later, when this deception was unmasked, the people of Israel demanded a retraction by the princes, but because they had put God's name on the decision, the elders were forced to honor the treaty.

In short order, five kings joined forces to come against Gibeon to destroy them for making peace with Israel. The Gibeonites sent word to Joshua that their defense was now his responsibility since they had become servants to Israel. Joshua had to defend those who were really his enemies because of the proud choice the princes had made.

Positional Authority Has Blinded Many Other Elders

Church leaders, whether pastors, elders, deacons, or whatever their titles might be, can be ever so earnest and dedicated and still make major mistakes. Sometimes it is in discipline; other times it is in enlarging the church facilities. Frequently, those in charge of selecting a new pastor are more impressed with degrees, charisma, or the recommendation of others than they are given to prayer and seeking God's will. The consequences can be long-term for the entire congregation.

Many years ago, I was asked to be a candidate to become the pastor of a church in the state of Washington. When meeting with the church board, they told me that my successful building program in my prior church had made them very interested in me. With an attitude of pride, they spoke of a choice piece of property they had purchased and on which they were preparing to build a new sanctuary.

"Did God lead you to this property" I asked? Not one of them could positively affirm that he had contacted God about the purchase. They were starting to describe the property when I asked them to wait a minute. I went to the blackboard and drew a description of the property. There was a small yellow house across the street at the back side of the apple orchard. This house had a tall flagpole with an oversized American flag flying on it.

"How did you know about this property?" they asked me.

"God showed it to me in a dream last night," I replied. "He also told me that your lawyer has not read the contract very thoroughly. There is a clause in the contract that allows the property to revert to the owner, who lives in the yellow house with the flag in front, as soon as your building is complete. The board members exchanged doubtful glances, but had to admit that my dream seemed otherwise accurate. During the next few days, they investigated and found that what I had said was true. If God had not graciously revealed this matter to me, they might have built a church that could legally have been taken away from them—however unethical the action might have been. As it turned out, I accepted their offer to be their pastor, and we never did build. We purchased a church building another congregation had outgrown.

Not too unlike Joshua's princes, we make personal choices in life without first consulting with God, and then we find we must live with the consequences of those choices for a long time. If we will allow ourselves to see this incident as an allegory, or even a parable, we can see how far pride in position can cause us to function outside of God's will—simply because we would not humble ourselves to ask God's advice.

The wisest man observed, *"In all thy ways acknowledge him, and he shall direct thy paths"* (Proverbs 3:6). Too frequently, we simply acknowledge God in what we classify as our "spiritual lives." King Solomon felt we should acknowledge God *"in all [our] ways."* This would include our married life, our child raising, our finances, and our personal relationships with others. This is not to renounce any personal responsibilities for decision making, but to acknowledge that God has veto power over any and all of our decisions. Like the child who says, "I'll be there if my mother will let me come," we keep all decisions subject to God's approval. If you are determined to function this way, I can guarantee you a battle with personal pride.

Pride in Position in Life Blinds Young People in Their Choices

Perhaps the two most important decisions made in our lives—career choices and the choice of marriage partners—are made by young people who have very little experience to fall back on. In our youth, we feel that we know "all things." We make choices based on our very limited resources and feel proud to be sufficiently mature enough to be allowed to make them.

Take the matter of a career choice. Many young Christians are guided into a career by a college counselor who bases his or her choice on the aptitudes, abilities, and apparent interests of the individual. Rather than ask the Lord what He has in mind for their lives, these young Christians often make a prideful decision that traps them in a field that leads to a dead-end job, one that proves to be very unfulfilling.

I've talked with many persons who admit that the particular subjects they pursued in college have proven useless in life. Some ministers spent years getting a commercial degree before hearing the call of God to the ministry. What a waste of time, energy, and resources! God knew all along that He intended for those individuals to be in the ministry, but they never asked Him about their life's career.

An even more important decision in life is the choice of a marriage partner. Far too few young people really seek the will of God in making this choice. Instead, they respond to the churning of their hormones and what they think they know about a person they believe they love. Little wonder that the divorce rate among American Christians is even higher than among unbelievers! Divine wisdom is available to us, but it is too often unsought, unwanted, or unheeded. As a consequence, many live in an unhappy relationship like Israel did with the Gibeonites. Their pride in making their decision by interpreting their feelings and going by what they saw in the natural may well have prevented a much better union God could have arranged for them.

Pride in Position Blinds Many Christians in the Handling of Their Finances

Can this story of the pride of Israel's princes be applied to the handling of our financial matters? Some Christians feel that they know better than God how to manage their money. I have observed, through years of pastoring, that when we substitute a tip for the tithe of our income, we evidence a pride that says, "I can handle my finances without God's help." Unfortunately, nontithers have no scriptural claims on God's financial provision. They are on their own. Tithing can have long-term effects, not only on our lives, but on the lives of our children as well.

One of Satan's greatest deceptions in the financial realm is the lie that we can buy now and pay later with no consequences. As a result, installment credit card debt has some Christians mortgaged beyond the Second Coming of Jesus. Somehow we become so proud of having such a lavish line of credit made available to us that we use it as cash without realizing the tremendous additional cost the interest adds to the purchase price. The turmoil this burden of debt creates can destroy personal peace and cause extreme anxiety, and it is a frequent cause of divorces. None of this is needful. Ask God for His wisdom before signing credit contracts.

Am I totally against the use of credit? Of course not. There are major purchases to be made, and most people must depend on a lending institution to make them. However, even these major purchases can have deception in them. Why not put our pride aside and seek the will of God before purchasing a house, a car, or any other major item? Sometimes our motive for acquiring property is impure. It may be merely to feed our pride. The key to merchandising in America is to make consumers dissatisfied with their possessions long before they are worn out. We Christians need not fall for this deception.

When we seek God's counsel before entering into a major purchase, we're sometimes nudged to remodel, get a new paint job, or have an engine overhauled. Other times, God gives us His approval for the purchase we are contemplating. How relaxing it will be in the years to come to realize that we're not putting up with a heavy liability we are doomed to endure; we're enjoying God's provision!

Positional Authority Often Makes Parents Dangerously Proud

Another area where pride in position may cause us to act unilaterally instead of bilaterally with God is in rearing our children. Is there any higher level of pride than that which parents experience while holding their baby? We enjoy having absolute authority over children, even though it sometimes needs to be enforced, for we want the very best in life for them.

Our initial success in directing the lives of these early adolescents can create a real pride in our parenting skills. How desperately we need to remember that we have very little advanced training for parenting! Instead, we get on-the-job training. We learn mostly through trial and error. As parents, we deal with eternal beings whose temporal destiny is in our hands and whose concepts of their divine destiny will be shaped by us. Are we really up to the task? Wouldn't some divine help be appreciated?

Fortunately, we need not be alone in raising our children. Our Creator God is available as our Counselor. He has given much guidance in His book, the Bible, and He is always willing to talk with us about our household problems. We need to ignore our pride as parents and go to God—admitting that we are not much beyond childhood ourselves. We should ask for divine wisdom for each child, for what works well with one child may not work at all for another.

As a pastor, I counseled and prayed with many parents whose children were breaking their hearts by their lifestyles. "We did the best we knew how," was a standard comment. Obviously, the choices a child makes determines the course of his life in spite of our training (look at Cain and Abel). I have often wondered how different the story might have been if those parents had humbly admitted to God their inability to *"train up a child in the way he should go,"* and had asked for help, wisdom, and grace for the task.

Joshua and the princes had a lifetime to regret having made a major decision on their own. They were seriously deceived by visible circumstances that were distorted in favor of the enemy. We will be, too, unless we habitually turn to God in our times of decision, and see if He vetoes or approves of our choices.

We, obviously, see only today's circumstances, while God sees into eternity. In looking backward, we can easily see that all of God's choices have been good for us. Isn't it likely that His present choices will prove to be the best for our lives as well?

Dear Father,

I honestly believe that the positions I hold in my home, on my job, and in the church have been ordained by You. Please help me to humble myself in fulfilling these roles. I know how gullible I am to flattery and other wiles of the devil. Sometimes my pride blinds me to what is obvious to others. Help me to discredit my pride and walk submissive to You in everything You have ordained for me to do, for You have promised, "In all thy ways acknowledge him, and he shall direct thy paths" (Proverbs 3:6). Right now I acknowledge that You are Lord of my life. I commit all my roles of leadership to You. Please direct me. Where my pride has caused me to make wrong decisions, please forgive me. In mercy and grace turn these things around for Your glory and for my good.

In Jesus' name,
Amen!

• • •

Questions

1. Think of a time when you were deceived, and evaluate your willingness to ask for help. How does pride contribute to our vulnerability to deception?

2. On a scale of one to ten, evaluate your willingness to ask for help as a general rule.

3. What regrets do you have in your life because you did not ask for help? When did you ask for God's direction?

4. Who helps you to make decisions?

5. How has pride interfered with your sound judgment?

Chapter 12

PRIDE AND CONTROL

When Israel became strong, they pressed the Canaanites into forced labor but never drove them out completely.

Judges 1:28, NIV

The angel of the Lord went up from Gilgal to Bokim and said, "I brought you up out of Egypt and led you into the land that I swore to give to your forefathers. I said, 'I will never break my covenant with you, and you shall not make a covenant with the people of this land, but you shall break down their altars.' Yet you have disobeyed me. Why have you done this? Now therefore I tell you that I will not drive them out before you; they will be [thorns] in your sides and their gods will be a snare to you."

Judges 2:1-3, NIV

*W*hen will God's people actually learn that partial obedience is classified by God as disobedience? God rebuked Israel's first king for disobedience through the prophet Samuel. Saul insisted that he had complied with God's instructions—at least partially. He cited the areas where he had obeyed God, and blamed the people in the areas of his disobedience. God's word to him was, *"Behold, to obey is better than sacrifice, and to hearken than the fat of rams. For rebellion is as the sin of witchcraft, and stubbornness is as iniquity and idolatry. Because thou hast rejected the word of the LORD, he hath also rejected thee from being king"* (1 Samuel 15:22-23). This partial obedience, which God called disobedience, cost Saul his kingdom, and this same mistake has cost many pastors their positions of authority.

The punishment Saul suffered for his disobedience may seem particularly harsh, but as the first king Saul was to be an example to others. He had a powerful example of God's attitude toward partial obedience in his forefathers as they entered the Promised Land. God prohibited Israel from making a league with any of the inhabitants of the land—complete destruction was God's policy. He wanted to eradicate idolatry from the land.

The first disobedience to this command was in the league Joshua and the princes made with Gibeon. Their pride got in the way of sound judgment. They were deceived and did not ask counsel of the Lord. The next sidestepping of God's orders is shown here in the beginning of the book of Judges. Israel did not completely destroy the inhabitants of the land. They conquered only as much territory as they needed in order to settle in comfortably. In Judges 2:3, God pointed out His displeasure with the exemption from death Israel extended to the Canaanites. He identified it as prideful disobedience.

Why had the people of Israel done this? Did they fear that God was unable to conquer this nation? Were Dagon and Asherah, whom the Canaanites served, stronger and greater than Jehovah? Maybe the Canaanites fought better and harder than the other nations the Israelites had already successfully conquered on their way to the Promised Land. It may have seemed the price was too great to continue struggling with the people. What proud unbelief!

God Has A Timetable

It is most likely that Israel merely postponed the final conquest. Having learned how valuable the Gibeonites had become as servants, more than likely they felt that another nation of slaves would also be beneficial. Perhaps, in their pride, Israel felt that she could eradicate these Canaanites any time she chose. Unfortunately, God's gift of conquest was at the entering of the land, not years later.

In ways we may not fully understand, God always has a timetable for His actions. If we don't move when God is moving, we will be left behind and may never catch up. There was a divine anointing for conquering the land when the people entered with Joshua. That anointing was never repeated, although Israel struggled with the Canaanites repeatedly throughout her history.

Many years ago, when I was still pastoring, God dealt severely with an area of my carnal nature that I enjoyed sufficiently to hold onto strongly. I would subdue it; then it would rise up and control me again. One day a prayer warrior came to my office from the prayer room with a message from God. It was very simple, but extremely powerful. God said, "Judson, this is the last time I will deal with you about this thing." This scared me into taking two days and a night for prayer...until, with God's help, I was able to bring that fleshly appetite to the cross of Christ.

When we first come to the Lord, there seems to be ample divine power available to overcome sin in our personal lives. Sinful habits, attitudes, actions, and lusts are so easily conquered and eradicated from our lives when the first rays of God's redemptive love shine upon us. The longer we wait, however, the more difficult it seems to be able to conquer them, until some Christians choose to live with these enemies rather than battle them.

The sin of the Israelites was that when they were able to obey God's direction, they pridefully set it aside in favor of a policy of their own. This was a direct disobedience, but it likely was disguised in the name of prudence or expediency. They knew God had given them power over the Canaanites, so they sought to control them and use them for their own convenience and service.

In spite of all of God's dealings with Israel, she seems to have failed to detest idolatry. She was so proud of her relationship with God that she didn't fear the idols of Canaan. Except for Joshua and Caleb, this generation had never been around idolatry. They had not lived in Egypt. They had lived their entire lives under the theocracy of Jehovah. They had no personal point of reference to see real harm in letting the Canaanites live among them, especially since they had been reduced to slaves. Pride caused them to think more of their own interests than of being obedient to God's will.

Obedience Must Match God's Gifts

The people of Israel had already taken possession of many of God's earthly gifts, but had rejected His word. They showed themselves to be self-seeking, greedy, carnal, and forgetful of the very One from whom they had received everything. It was the old story of personal pride slipping into the place of obedience to God—the old partial obedience syndrome at work again.

The pride of this people in believing that they could easily control the enemy was rooted in unbelief. The same unbelief that kept their fathers from entering this land was now preventing them from fully conquering it. Half-conquered territory never brings glory to God, but it consistently brings grief to Christians.

How characteristic this desire to control instead of destroy is of the lives of many Christians! We prefer to live with old enemies rather than exert the effort to bring them to the cross to be destroyed. Some persons overapply Paul's statement, *"For sin shall not be your master, because you are not under law, but under grace"* (Romans 6:14, NIV). This is a provision, but it is not an automatic reality. We need to balance this verse with Galatians 5:24: *"Those who belong to Christ Jesus have crucified the sinful nature with its passions and desires"* (NIV). We wrestle with sinful tendencies, passions, and lusts until we can get them on the cross with Jesus. But halfway crucifixion doesn't count. Dragging the severely wounded sinful nature off the cross and nursing it back to health is not only stupid; it is potentially disastrous. When it gets well, it will try to get even, but without the mercy you have shown to it.

Like the Israelites who could have conquered the Canaanites, we, too, often feel that control is sufficient. We keep our lusts, sinful habits, and unholy passions under control most of the time, but when they get the upper hand, even if for only a short season, they often do irreparable damage—both to us and to others through us.

In a previous century, Matthew Henry wrote, "Self-indulgence, a love of ease, and present worldly advantages, both spring from and foster unbelief. Thus many a sinner, who seems to have escaped Satan's bondage, is entangled again, and his last state is worse than the first. Many a believer who begins well is hindered—he grows negligent and afraid of the cross. His grace languishes, his lusts revive, Satan plies him with suitable temptations, the world recovers its hold; he brings guilt into his conscience, anguish into his heart, discredit upon his character, and reproach for the Gospel."[1]

Death, Not Compromise, Is God's Provision for Carnal Flesh

How easily we, like Israel, rationalize living with enemies rather than destroying them. Usually we can see some service they can provide for us. The smoker feels it gives him comfort to take time to smoke a cigarette. Many Christians say that having a drink or two relaxes them in the evening. They are forgetting the terror their former addiction to alcohol was to them and to everyone close to them. Still others like to have an evening at a casino gambling "for relaxation." Isn't this a bit like playing with rattlesnakes for excitement? Similarly, we take pleasure in the gossip and backbiting that are so accepted socially, but are abominations to God. He hates these sins!

The Christian man viewing pornography on a website rationalizes that he is enjoying sexual pleasure without hurting anyone. What a damnable lie from the devil this has become! This private practice has destroyed hundreds of Christian marriages, ruined pastors' ministries, and put many believers' lives under the bondage of lust.

All who are involved in these practices (and many more illustrations could be given) declare that they can quit anytime they want to. They, like Israel, have put these carnal desires under tribute in a proud attitude that such desires can be controlled. Like Israel, they wake up one day to discover that these passions are actually controlling *them*.

The angel of the Lord told Israel, *"Now therefore I tell you that I will not drive them out before you; they will be thorns in your sides and their gods will be a snare to you"* (Judges 2:3, NIV). When pride prevents us from fully obeying the Word of God, we may find ourselves completely on our own in dealing with our enemies. Our pride may have made us feel we could expel these enemy forces whenever we wanted, but without the help of the angel of the Lord we cannot conquer anything. Israel's strength was never in her armed might; it was always in the presence of Jehovah fighting for and with her. And so it is with us.

After the angel told them that God was displeased with their disobedience and would not drive out these Canaanites, *"the people lifted up their voice, and wept. And they called the name of that place Bochim ['weepers']: and they sacrificed there unto the LORD"* (Judges 2:4-5). Unfortunately, no amount of weeping and sacrifice changed God's mind.

As God told King Saul, *"Behold, to obey is better than sacrifice, and to hearken than the fat of rams. For rebellion is as the sin of witchcraft, and stubbornness is as iniquity and idolatry"* (1 Samuel 15:22-23).

If I have sounded legalistic and narrow-minded in my application of this passage of Scripture, I am sorry. It's just that during the seventy years I have been preaching, I have seen the great contrast between those who make a full confession of sin at conversion and allow the cross of Christ to thoroughly cleanse their lives and those who seek to merely add God to their lives. They try desperately to keep everything under control, but they eventually lose the battle.

Thousands of people here in America have "come to the altar," but then they have quickly returned to the ways of the world. They may classify themselves as Christians, but there is only the fruit of worldliness and selfishness in their lives. They have chosen to live with the Canaanites for what they can get from them, little knowing that these heathen will eventually control their lives. We need to beware of the pride of trying to subjugate what God said to eradicate. God has not told us to control the lusts of the flesh; He said to kill them!

Holiness Affects Our Behavior As Well As Our Beliefs

God has abundant and beautiful places to bring us into, but we must be clean and holy to possess them. It is the holy life that is a powerful life, and God has made a measure of His holiness available to us. He starts by cleansing us from the unholy things the world system deposited in us before we were saved. The cross slays the old sinful nature, and the blood of Jesus cleanses us from the defilement that nature left in us. The promise of the Scripture is, *"If we confess our sins, he is faithful and just to forgive us our sins, and to cleanse us from all unrighteousness"* (1 John 1:9).

We must resist the prideful partial or selective obedience in letting go of the ways of the world. The words of the prophet Micah to Israel might well be spoken to Christians in this twenty-first century: *"Get up, go away! For this is not your resting place, because it is defiled, it is ruined, beyond all remedy"* (Micah 2:10, NIV). This is not a time for compromise with the world. It is a time for cleansing from the defilement of the world that we might be examples of righteousness and holiness to our generation.

Endnote:

1. Matthew Henry, *Commentary on the Holy Bible*, Vol. I, (Nashville: Thomas Nelson Inc., 1979).

Dear Jesus,

I have to admit that You seem to want to take away from me many things that I thought would be useful to me—even necessary for me. Please help me to see that I don't need to make slaves of what You have condemned to death. You can do more for me than they ever could. Lord, when I look back on my Christian walk, I see so many areas of partial obedience. Please forgive me. I really do want to walk in complete obedience to Your Word, no matter what it may cost me. Help me to bring my pride of self-control to the cross and crucify it there with You. Maybe I'll have to do it daily, but it will be worth it. Please help me or I'll be out of control.

Thank You.
Amen!

• • •

Questions

1. In what areas of your life are you tempted to compromise?

2. In what specific way is proud unbelief the root of compromise?

3. What would you say to a person who is asking for your help to stop compromising?

Chapter 13

PRIDE AND PERFORMANCE

*Again the Israelites did evil in the eyes of the L*ORD*, so the L*ORD *delivered them into the hands of the Philistines for forty years. A certain man of Zorah, named Manoah, from the clan of the Danites, had a wife who was sterile and remained childless. The angel of the L*ORD *appeared to her and said, "You are sterile and childless, but you are going to conceive and have a son. Now see to it that you drink no wine or other fermented drink and that you do not eat anything unclean, because you will conceive and give birth to a son. No razor may be used on his head, because the boy is to be a Nazirite, set apart to God from birth, and he will begin the deliverance of Israel from the hands of the Philistines."*
Judges 13:1-5, NIV

*The woman gave birth to a boy and named him Samson. He grew and the L*ORD *blessed him, and the Spirit of the L*ORD *began to stir him while he was in Mahaneh Dan, between Zorah and Eshtaol.*
Judges 13:24-25, NIV

*The Spirit of the L*ORD *came upon him in power so that he tore the lion apart with his bare hands as he might have torn a young goat. But he told neither his father nor his mother what he had done.*
Judges 14:6, NIV

*Then the Spirit of the L*ORD *came upon him in power.*
Judges 14:19, NIV

*As he approached Lehi, the Philistines came toward him shouting. The Spirit of the L*ORD *came upon him in power. The ropes on his arms became like charred flax, and the bindings dropped from his hands. Finding a fresh jawbone of a donkey, he grabbed it and struck down a thousand men.*
Judges 15:14-15, NIV

Samson led [judged, KJV] Israel for twenty years in the days of the Philistines.
Judges 15:20, NIV

"If you don't conquer them now, they'll conquer you later," was the essence of what God told the Israelites when they entered the Promised Land under Joshua's leadership. How true this proved to be. Rather than remain subdued, these subjugated enemies strengthened themselves as they multiplied, and they repeatedly came against the people of Israel and put them into subjection. God often said that He allowed this to happen because Israel had turned from serving Jehovah.

After a season of chastisement, the people cried out to God and He raised up a deliverer to rally Israel to throw off the yoke of bondage. Usually this deliverer became the ruler of Israel under the title of judge. The last of these judges was Samson.

Samson was the twelfth judge. He was unique among the others, for God set him apart for his task even before his conception. He was one of the few men in the Bible who took a lifetime Nazirite vow, although he treated it with a casualness amounting to contempt.

Samson came on the scene when the Philistines were very much in control of Israel, not through armed conflict, but through trade and commerce. I don't know that this would have been so distressing to God except that the worship of Baal came with this link. God raised up Samson to make coexistence with the Philistines less comfortable and Baal worship detestable.

More space is given in the Bible to Samson and his exploits than is given to any other judge. There was never anyone else like Samson. He was a conundrum and a mixture. Books have been written about him, including one that I wrote. We have neither biblical nor historical evidence that Samson was unusually large, but when the Spirit of

God came upon him, he became abnormally strong. He was lustful after what the Bible elsewhere calls "strange flesh." He liked Philistine women far better than the Israelite ladies.

He was a formidable and unconquerable force as long as he stayed, even loosely, within the restrictions of his Nazirite vow. Although his lusts repeatedly got him into trouble, his anointing easily got him out of it—often very dramatically. This seems to have induced a high level of pride in his performance.

A supernatural anointing of God consistently tends to cause the anointed person to become proud of what he could do with that anointing. I chose to call this "performance pride." There are at least four commonalities about performance pride: (1) It wants to be seen. (2) It is usually a solo act. (3) It often compromises the consecration that induced the anointing. (4) It is very self-serving. Look at these four elements in Samson.

Performance Pride Wants to Be Seen

Samson's first display of power was killing a lion with his bare hands. It happened in private, but he couldn't let it remain unknown. He formed it into a riddle that ruined his wedding feast. He didn't just slip out of town when he found himself trapped in Gaza, the chief city of the Philistines (after spending a night with a prostitute there). As he was leaving, he picked up the gates of the city and carried them to Hebron, Israel's chief city, about thirty-seven miles away. It seems that everything Samson did was done with a flair that drew attention to himself. He was, indeed, the great one, and no one could top his deeds.

While an anointing that produced physical strength similar to Samson's does not seem to have been repeated in the Bible, such pride in performance is all too common today. Some gifted and anointed persons seem to want others to realize how great their gift is. For example, once, when I was introduced as the guest speaker at a church one Sunday morning, the associate pastor stepped to the microphone ahead of me. He made an appeal for anyone who had a problem they wanted God to solve to come and stand in the front. Once they were lined up, he told them to raise their hands. Then he gestured toward them from one end of the line to the other, all the while crying loudly, "Be healed." Everyone in the line fell down "under the power." The young man then turned to me and said, "Let's see you top that!" I wasn't interested in trying to match anointings; I had come to deliver the Word of God to the congregation.

I've ministered in conferences where the speakers seemed to be competing with one another, each trying to top the other rather than flow in the Spirit to complete what God was saying at the time. This is nothing less than performance pride, and it often becomes very odious.

This same performance pride is often seen in our Christian musicians. Some of them have come to Christ from the worldly entertainment field. They are so used to selling themselves while performing their music that they often bring this attitude into the Church. Even Christian musicians who were raised in the Church feel pressured to be performers rather than worshipers with their music. It seems more important that they be seen, recognized, and remembered than that they bring the blessing of God to the believers.

Since the dance has been returned to the Church as a legitimate expression of worship, I have seen dancers releasing their souls in beautiful worship, often with tears streaming down their faces. I have also seen dancers putting on a performance that drew attention to themselves instead of to God. Performance pride may be expressed in a variety of ways, but if it is present, it will be seen.

Why is it necessary to call attention to the special gifting God may have given to us? Are we running for office, or do we live on the adrenaline pubic praise can generate? Jesus clearly said that the Holy Spirit would not call attention to Himself, but that He would glorify the Son. Why can't we do the same? Why is it important for people to know that it was when we preached, prayed, or testified that dramatic things happened? As Samson later learned, without the Holy Spirit, we would have been a complete failure. Why, then, do we seek to take credit for what He has done?

Performance Pride Is Usually a Solo Act

The judges who preceded Samson rallied the men and women of Israel to join in the attack against their oppressors. Not so with Samson. Although he ruled as judge in Israel for twenty years, we have no record of his ever bringing anyone else into his battles with the Philistines. Samson's was a solo act. His pride convinced him that he didn't need the help of anyone else.

Performers realize that if they share the act, they must share the glory. God isn't as interested in raising up Samsons as He is in maturing His Church for action. His Word says of Jesus: *"It was he who gave some to be apostles, some to be prophets, some to be evangelists, and some to be pastors and teachers, to prepare God's people for works of service, so that the body of Christ may be built up"* (Ephesians 4:11-12, NIV). Our leaders are to prepare believers for Christian service. Samson never did this, and many Christian leaders today are as guilty as he. It sometimes seems easier to do the task ourselves than to prepare another to do it, but God's work is scheduled for the Body of believers, not for solo ministries.

The American Church is so accustomed to great performers functioning as solo acts that we make heroes of these men and women and follow them from conference to conference. They, for the most part, are not building a body of believers or even contributing to Christ's Church. They are calling attention to their abilities, giftings, and anointings in solo performances on the Christian stage and television. Their ministry is gone forever when they pass on, for they have not trained Timothys to carry on the work. Solo acts cannot be passed on to others, but plural ministry can. Maybe we don't need titled church officers in fancy robes and clerical collars as much as we need Spirit-filled men and women who will train believers for their work of ministry.

Performance Pride Often Compromises Consecration

The book of Judges leaves no room to question Samson's unique commission to be a deliverer. From his birth to his death, the Spirit of the Lord came upon Samson to do great feats of deliverance. There was, however, one qualification. Samson was to live the Nazirite vow for life. It is obvious that this great man played very fast and loose with his vow. He violated the prohibition of touching a dead body in eating honey from the slain lion, and in the killing of thousands of Philistines. It is difficult to believe he participated in his seven-day wedding feast without joining others in drinking. The only provision in this vow that Samson seemed to hold sacred was his uncut hair—the outer, visible aspect of his vow.

As long as this outward evidence of his Nazirite vow remained untouched, Samson seemed content to live a rather salacious, lustful life. Only once in the narrative do we see him in relationship with the people of Israel—when the men of Judah bound him and delivered him to the Philistines. All other relationships shown were with the enemy. He fraternized with the very persons God purposed for him to destroy.

One commentator wrote: "But does the presence of God's Spirit imply anything about his moral character? Samson was tempted in the area of his weakness, and he sometimes used his power without much thought for righteousness or justice (e.g., Judges 14:19; 15:14, 19; cf. 16:19, 28, 30).

"But there were also occasions when Samson did call upon God (15:18; 16:28), and God's response implies that Samson was sincere in his entreaty. In this, Samson differed from his contemporaries, and for this the New Testament includes his name among the heroes of faith (Hebrews 11:32)"[1]

It seems to be increasingly common for a person carrying a ministerial anointing from God to use it as proof that God approves of his or her lifestyle. Loved by many, but responsible to none, many solo-act Christian performers come to believe that they are above, or, at least, an exception to, the law. They satisfy their greed, lusts, and egos however they will and do not expect to be penalized for it. Repeatedly, when dealing with ministers involved with immorality, I have been told, "But all the time I was involved, the anointing of God was heavy upon my ministry."

God's anointing for ministry is never to be taken as approval of a lifestyle. As F.F. Bruce writes, "A Charismatic anointing in the Old Testament period did not necessarily produce purity of life. God could still make use of a person apart from the quality of his life. Amongst his unlikely instruments were Balaam, Nebuchadnezzar, and Cyrus. We may question his use of an agent like Samson, and be embarrassed by the details, but God is sovereign, and he used Samson, in the 'Dark Ages' of the Judges' period, to fulfill a lone but vital role."[2]

Being able to raise the dead is not a sign of divine approval of a lifestyle that is beneath the New Testament standard. To plead the presence of power as an excuse for impure living is asking for the judgment of God. God has always been more interested in what we *are* than in what we *can do*. Samson was used by God because no one else was available, but Samson lost his life in finally fulfilling God's commission. He brought down the whole house of Dagon upon himself and everyone around him. This is still being done today by Samson-like ministers upon whom the roof finally caves in—destroying their entire kingdoms and many of their faithful followers.

Eerdman's Handbook to the Bible reminds us, "Moral weakness robs the strong man of both spiritual stature and physical prowess—since his strength is God-given for a specific purpose."[3] Was this true of Samson only? Have not many anointed men and women also lost their spiritual stature and even their health because of moral weakness?

Performance Pride Is Self-serving

Samson was brought into this world specially anointed to deliver Israel. The facts of his life show that every display of divine power was used to deliver Samson, not Israel. His folly got him into trouble with the Philistines, and God's anointing got him out of it. Samson seemed to lack compassion for his people, but he had great passion for his own needs, and he consistently used God's power to help him fulfill those needs.

Some years ago, I knew a minister with a precious gift of bringing God's presence into a congregation of people. I gravitated to him...until I realized that he was very self-serving. Eventually he founded a church in an American city and very openly began to convince people, especially those with money, to leave their churches and come to his. I couldn't believe how people uprooted their families and moved thousands of miles to be with him. The real reason for establishing this church was to provide money for his widespread family, and the touch of God upon his life opened people's hearts and wallets for many years. Eventually, this house also collapsed—leaving wounded and dying believers in the rubble.

Throughout the Old Testament, I do not see a true prophet of God using his gift in a self-serving manner. I see Elisha's servant doing this, but he was smitten with leprosy for it. Unfortunately, I now see too many modern prophets serving themselves with God's gifts. The Samson performance pride is always self-serving, when, in fact, all our anointings should be used to serve the Body of Christ here on earth.

Endnotes:

1. *The International Standard Bible Encyclopedia*, Vol. IV (Grand Rapids, Mich.: William B. Eerdmans Publishing Co., 1979).
2. IBID
3. *Eerdman's Handbook to the Bible* (Herds, England: Lion Publishing, 1973).

Dear Jesus,

I never cease being amazed at what the Holy Spirit can do through the man or woman who will surrender to You, but I get hurt to the point of anger when I see such men and women performing like a three-ring circus, calling much attention to themselves. Please forgive me, Lord, for I realize that this performance pride is in me, too. I like people to know that God is using me, and, I fear, there are times when what I do is also self-serving. Please help me to perform my vows completely and live a holy life uncontaminated by self-promotion.

Thank You.
Amen!

• • •

Questions

1. Who is a Timothy in your life into whose life you are sowing?

2. Samson was not a good steward of God's anointing. What helps us steward the Holy Spirit's power?

3. In one or two sentences, state the message of this chapter in your own words.

4. Why is Samson such a popular person in the Bible?

5. Which of the four commonalties of performance pride is the biggest challenge in your life (see page 121): (1) must be seen (2) is usually a solo act (3) often compromises (4) is self-serving.

Chapter 14

PRIDE AND ARROGANCE

Saul answered [Samuel], "But am I not a Benjamite, from the smallest tribe of Israel, and is not my clan the least of all the clans of the tribe of Benjamin? Why do you say such a thing to me?" 1 Samuel 9:21, NIV

Then Samuel took a flask of oil and poured it on Saul's head and kissed him, saying, "Has not the LORD anointed you leader over his inheritance?" 1 Samuel 10:1, NIV

"The Spirit of the LORD will come upon you in power, and you will prophesy with them; and you will be changed into a different person. Once these signs are fulfilled, do whatever your hand finds to do, for God is with you" 1 Samuel 10:6-7, NIV

As Saul turned to leave Samuel, God changed Saul's heart, and all these signs were fulfilled that day. 1 Samuel 10:9, NIV

*7*he story of Saul, Israel's first king, is all too illustrative of the rise and fall of spiritual leaders—from the top level on down. Saul didn't seek the position and was shocked when Samuel anointed him to be king over all Israel. He hid himself at coronation time and had to be sought out. Although he was taller than any other Israelite, he was extremely aware of his humble origins. He told Samuel that he came from Israel's smallest tribe, Benjamin, and his family was the least of all the families in that tribe. It became necessary for God to change his heart—even change him into a different man—before he could accept this challenge. This kind of humility touches the heart of God.

When I see the proud arrogance of some Christian leaders today, I am comforted to know they were not like that when God called them, for James says: *"God opposes the proud but gives grace to the humble"* (James 4:6, NIV). Jesus said, *"Whosoever shall exalt himself shall be abased; and he that shall humble himself shall be exalted"* (Matthew 23:12). No, God does not call the person with an exorbitant estimation of self-worth, insolence, haughtiness, and loftiness into the Gospel ministry. Some such persons may be self-appointed, but most of the proud became that way long after God has called them into divine service.

Initially, those whom God calls into any realm of Christian service are given a "new heart," as was Saul. Often the prophetic voice comes to and through them, and they are *"turned into another man,"* just as happened to Saul the Benjamite. By God's choice, these people bring grace and humility into His service, but, too frequently, the office changes the person. Early successes produce a personal pride that often leads to arrogance. Those who suffer this evil often don't seem to realize that wearing a halo too tight gives others a headache.

Saul did not become arrogant overnight, and neither do we. From the day he was anointed to be king until God slew him in battle nearly forty years later, Saul's pride grew from one level to another. God put him through several humiliating experiences, hoping that he would humble his heart, but apart from God's help, pride is not easily slain.

Pride's Arrogance in Attitude

Long before others see the pride in us, it has taken root as an attitude within us. All action begins as an attitude, which is probably why Jesus warned us, *"For from within, out of men's hearts, come evil thoughts, sexual immorality, theft, murder, adultery, greed, malice, deceit, lewdness, envy, slander, arrogance and folly. All these evils come from inside and make a man 'unclean' "* (Mark 7:21-23, NIV).

Since God changed Saul's heart before he became king, all his destructive attitudes had to come after this change. Isn't that consistent with our own experience? We are cleansed and renewed at conversion, but we subsequently allow pride to bring back into us many of the traits the blood of Jesus had cleansed from our lives. This process is often so slow and steady that we are unaware of what is being produced in us.

This seems to have been Saul's problem. In his second year as king, the Philistines came against Israel with a formidable force. Saul led a fearful army of Hebrews out to meet them, but his men began to desert and hide in caves and in the rocks. Samuel had agreed to meet Saul and the army at Gilgal in seven days to offer a sacrifice and intercede for God's help. Samuel seemed to be late in arriving, and Saul felt it expedient to take on the office of priest and offer the sacrifice himself (see 1 Samuel 13:9). He explained to Samuel, *"I forced myself therefore, and offered a burnt offering"* (1 Samuel 13:12). In just two years, his pride had risen to such arrogance that he dared to take on the office of priest as well as that of king.

Pride and Arrogance

Later in Israel's history, other kings such as Uzziah tried to function as priests, but always with severe penalties from God. God guards His appointments. It is not the will of God that one person be all things. The attitude "I can do it all" is arrogant and displeasing to God. We need one another, and no matter how efficiently we may be able to fulfil our office or calling, we dare not try to take another's place in the Body of Christ. Saul was the king; Samuel was the prophet. They needed each other, but neither could replace the other.

Another area of Saul's attitudes that reveals the arrogance his pride had generated was his relationship with David. Early in Saul's reign, David was God's channel for removing the tormenting evil spirits from the king. Later, David delivered Israel from the Philistines by slaying their giant, Goliath. The Bible tells us that David was a faithful servant to Saul, but his popularity with the people aroused a dangerous jealousy in the king. This jealousy enlarged into a murderous rage that lasted for years. David had to run for his life, and only God's protection prevented Saul from killing him.

If jealousy and pride are not twin brothers, they are at least first cousins. This form of arrogant pride is dangerously common in Christian circles today. Singers in the choir become jealous of the soloist. Youth directors are jealous of the senior pastor, and sometimes the senior pastor is jealous of the acclaim offered to the assistant pastor. Members of the congregation jealously vie with one another for attention, and among most church staffs there is an undercurrent of jealous behavior. There seems to be a constant jockeying for position and authority.

Seldom do we realize that the root of all this jealousy is pride. Arrogantly we feel that we are more deserving, more capable, and have more seniority than others. This exaggerated view of our own worth usually becomes overbearing, and sometimes even murderous. We may not kill the physical body, but we kill the reputation, the sense of self-worth, and the ministry of others—all because of an arrogant attitude.

Pride's Arrogance in Action

It takes more self-control than most of us possess to keep arrogant attitudes under control. What we think and feel begins to control what we do—sooner or later. Saul illustrates this principle, for Saul soon found it convenient to disobey God (and to partially obey Him). His attitude of "I know better than God" became an act of stubborn, willful insubordination.

Recently, a friend of mine, who was music director for a large church, was informed by his pastor that he was searching for a different pastorate. The music director wisely began to search for a place to go and interviewed successfully with an even larger church. When his pastor heard this, he angrily declared, "I don't want that, and I can stop it." He went to the phone and informed the pastor interested in hiring my friend that he would not release his music director. My friend and I and the interviewing pastor had all felt that this move by my friend was the will of God, but the pastor, who was preparing to leave his church, took God's role. By using religious politics, this pastor "killed" this young man's chances. What arrogance! What pride! How disastrous for this young man.

Unfortunately, "playing God" is far too common today. Our pride in position causes us to overestimate our worth in the Kingdom. I have said for years, "If you want to stay out of trouble with God, keep off His throne." This arrogance in action filters down from high-level religious circles to the home, where parents sometimes play the role of God in controlling the lives of their children. I know of too many examples where God called young persons into the ministry, but the parents insisted they train to enter other professions.

This arrogance of disobedience is seen in the way many Christians treat God's commands to tithe, to be witnesses, to gather together in worship sessions, and in their missionary vision. How audacious of any of us to pretend that we know better than God, but that is what partial obedience or all-out disobedience actually is. We are setting the rules instead of following them.

Pride and Arrogance

Saul's most arrogant action came when he consulted with the witch at Endor. God was not speaking to him, so in desperation he tried to contact the deceased Samuel, although witchcraft had always been forbidden in Israel (see Leviticus 19:31). In disguise, Saul set out at night on a dangerous journey to get close to the enemy camp at Shunem and to consult the medium at Endor. It is as though Saul told God, "If You won't speak to me through Urim and Thummin, I'll find someone who can give me a word from the spirit world." He did, but the message was very unwelcome. Samuel, called up from the grave, predicted Saul's death and Israel's defeat in battle.

When spiritual pride reaches the level of arrogance, almost anything will be done. Saul was convinced that he was an exception to God's rules because he was the king of Israel. Many Christians convince themselves that they, too, are exceptions to God's rules and prohibitions. Eventually, this causes God to cease speaking to them or, more accurately, they become deaf to the voice of God.

In times of desperation, those whose ears God has stopped will seek far and wide for "a word from the Lord." They will go to prophetic conventions and stand in line waiting their turn to have a prophetic word uttered over them. If they don't like that word, there is always another convention somewhere else to attend.

Please don't misunderstand me. I am not putting modern prophets in the category of a medium, but the principle seen in Saul is all too often activated in the lives of the arrogantly proud. When their pride and disobedience closes off communication with God, rather than repent and reestablish personal communication with Him, they commonly slip away in the quiet of the night to seek communication from the spirit world through someone else, or they place a long-distance phone call to their favorite spiritual communicator.

Pride's Arrogance in Self-appraisal

We've all seen our share of arrogantly proud Christians strutting like proud peacocks. Time and again, I have sat on platforms and found it easy to pick out the deacons just by the way they walked. Sometimes just a swish of the hips informed us all that a certain well-dressed lady was the wife of one of the deacons.

Some of our key ministers today consistently have an entourage surrounding them, and several have actually hired bodyguards to protect them. Just let a "common person" try to get near them, and they are quickly, and sometimes rudely, told that the great one cannot be disturbed. How thankful I am that Jesus didn't keep the people from Himself! He gladly ministered to them. On the one occasion the disciples tried to keep people (in this case, children) from coming to Him, Jesus soundly rebuked them.

It is likely that none of us are as important as we think we are. Paul warned us, *"For by the grace given me I say to every one of you: Do not think of yourself more highly than you ought, but rather think of yourself with sober judgment, in accordance with the measure of faith God has given you"* (Romans 12:3, NIV). The size of our church, the number of gifts we may have, the amount of income we make, or the success of our families is not the measurement God has imposed on us. His yardstick is the amount of faith He has entrusted to us. Since this faith is His gift, there is actually no basis for pride.

Pride is insidious. Not one of us is immune to it. We were nothings and nobodies until Christ came into our lives. Now we are *"heirs of God and co-heirs with Christ, if indeed we share in his sufferings in order that we may also share in his glory"* (Romans 8:17, NIV). How easy it is to forget that we share in *"his glory"!* It is not our own, and to bask in our own glory is forbidden.

The world needs us; the church needs us; our homes and families need us; but others cannot receive from an arrogantly proud person. Never forget that pride is the only disease that makes everyone sick except the one who has it.

Paul challenged us, *"Do nothing out of selfish ambition or vain conceit, but in humility consider others better than yourselves"* (Philippians 2:3, NIV). Put into action, this principle would take care of arrogant pride in our Christian walk and service.

Dear Jesus,

I so despise the arrogant pride I come in contact with so regularly, but am I free from it? Do I have too high an opinion of myself and of my ministry? If so, please make me aware of it and forgive me. I really do want to serve others, not be served by them. You have given to me in such boundless measure, and I want to distribute Your gifts wherever I go. Help me to not talk down to people or make them feel inferior in receiving from me.

Thank You.
Amen!

• • •

Questions

1. What are some ways we "play God"?

2. What are some ways we can humble ourselves? (For example, choose to serve others, receive correction, submit to authority, confess our sins.)

3. How do you identify with Saul? (For example, do you hide out of fear?)

Chapter 15

PRIDE'S SEPARATION

All this happened to King Nebuchadnezzar. Twelve months later, as the king was walking on the roof of the royal palace of Babylon, he said, "Is not this the great Babylon I have built as the royal residence, by my mighty power and for the glory of my majesty?"

The words were still on his lips when a voice came from heaven, "This is what is decreed for you, King Nebuchadnezzar: Your royal authority has been taken from you. You will be driven away from people and will live with the wild animals; you will eat grass like cattle. Seven times will pass by for you until you acknowledge that the Most High is sovereign over the kingdoms of men and gives them to anyone he wishes."

Immediately what had been said about Nebuchadnezzar was fulfilled. He was driven away from people and ate grass like cattle. His body was drenched with the dew of heaven until his hair grew like the feathers of an eagle and his nails like the claws of a bird.

At the end of that time, I, Nebuchadnezzar, raised my eyes toward heaven, and my sanity was restored. Then I praised the Most High; I honored and glorified him who lives forever. His dominion is an eternal dominion; his kingdom endures from generation to generation. All the peoples of the earth are regarded as nothing. He does as he pleases with the powers of heaven and the peoples of the earth. No one can hold back his hand or say to him: "What have you done?"

At the same time that my sanity was restored, my honor and splendor were returned to me for the glory of my kingdom. My advisers and nobles sought me out, and I was restored to my throne and became even greater than before. Now I, Nebuchadnezzar, praise and exalt and glorify the King of heaven, because everything he does is right and all his ways are just. And those who walk in pride he is able to humble.

Daniel 4:28-37, NIV

One of the classic examples of the separating power of pride is King Nebuchadnezzar, who reigned as king of Babylon for forty-three years. He was a brilliant military strategist who conquered all of Palestine in three separate campaigns. It was he who besieged Jerusalem, captured it, and eventually destroyed it completely. He brought the Davidic dynasty to an end. After his first capture of Jerusalem, he took the scholars and princes from Jerusalem to Babylon. These included Daniel (Belteshazzer), Shadrach, Meshach, and Abed-nego (their Persian names).

When God was foretelling His people Israel of their coming captivity, He said it would be accomplished by *"Nebuchadnezzar the king of Babylon, MY SERVANT"* (Jeremiah 25:9, 27:6, emphasis mine). This underscores the fact that God can use anyone to do anything to fulfill the divine purpose. Nebuchadnezzar was so important in God's plan that he is mentioned about ninety times in the Old Testament.

For a heathen king who had taken the treasures of the house of God and displayed them in the temple of his own gods, Nebuchadnezzar was given great mercy by Jehovah. Not only did God allow this king great power of conquest, He seems also to have given him distinguished architectural skills. Babylon was beautiful beyond imagination, and the king's hanging gardens have long been listed among the seven wonders of the world. Furthermore, he must have possessed outstanding managerial skills to hold together such a far-flung kingdom.

Twice, God gave Nebuchadnezzar prophetic dreams, and both times Daniel interpreted them accurately. When Nebuchadnezzar angrily threw the three Hebrews into the fiery furnace for praying to Jehovah instead of to him, he was allowed to see a theophanic manifestation of Jesus in the furnace with these men. After this incident, Nebuchadnezzar issued a decree prohibiting anyone from speaking against Jehovah, and ended the declaration by saying, *"No other god can save in this way"* (Daniel 3:29, NIV). In short, Nebuchadnezzar was a heathen king chosen by Jehovah as a servant to punish Israel and to whom God gave several manifestations of Himself and of His power.

Reading the historical accounts and comparing them with the Bible account, it would seem that Nebuchadnezzar was almost perfect. There had been no one so great before him, and few in history after him are qualified to stand in his shadow. He did have one flaw, however, and it was a serious one. He became extremely proud. When Daniel was talking to King Belshazzar, who followed Nebuchadnezzar to the throne, he reminded him, *"O king, the Most High God gave your father Nebuchadnezzar sovereignty and greatness and glory and splendor. Because of the high position he gave him, all the peoples and nations and men of every language dreaded and feared him. ... But when his heart became arrogant and HARDENED WITH PRIDE, he was deposed from his royal throne and stripped of his glory"* (Daniel 5:18-20, NIV, emphasis mine). Human pride tore down what God had built up! And it still does.

The story of Nebuchadnezzar, as told in both the historical and the prophetic books of the Old Testament, graphically illustrates at least four aspects of pride's power to separate. It separates us from our associates, from our true selves, from our "kingdom," and from our God.

Pride Separates Us From Our Associates

Nebuchadnezzar was brilliant, but he was not Superman. He needed an army for conquest, and counselors and governors to control what he had captured. He could not maintain his conquests without many helpers, but his pride built a wall of separation between himself and them. Eventually this pride drove him from his world.

Pride does the same thing in our lives. No one likes a proud man or woman, for he or she projects an air of superiority that is uncomfortable to be around. The very proud person alienates himself from friends, barricades himself from counsel, and ends up lonesome and emotionally bankrupt.

How often I have seen a pastor bring highly qualified staff members to work with him, only to alienate himself from them by high-level pride. It happens in the business world as well, and it has also been the real cause of many divorces. How well the wise man of the Bible knew this, for he wrote, *"Pride goes before destruction, a haughty spirit before a fall"* (Proverbs 16:18, NIV). We can't afford the luxury of pride, for we are not complete in ourselves. We need the help of others, and uncontrolled pride will separate us from them.

Pride Separates Us From Our True Selves

Nebuchadnezzar lost his mind, his sense of reason, and became so brutish that he was put out into the fields away from people. He lived in the open and ate grass for food like cattle. Twice, God says that this came upon him because of his pride—particularly the pride of taking credit for what God had done.

James S. Hewett says, "When the 'I' becomes dominant, the 'spiritual eye' sees the entire world in a distortion."[1] My experience shows that it is not only the "spiritual eye" that gets distorted; the entire view of life takes on a myopic distortion. We become extremely nearsighted. Since "I" is the very center of the word *prIde*, everything in life is filtered through this "I-centeredness." Our pride separates us from different views and concepts of life, limiting us to our own personal world. While we may become large in our own eyes, we actually prevent ourselves from developing and growing socially, intellectually, and spiritually.

Pride so distorts sound reasoning that it separates us from our true selves. In our pride, we think of ourselves more highly than we ought to think (which God prohibits—see Romans 12:3), and often find ourselves involved in activities that are far beyond our real capabilities. This, of course, is a perfect setup for failure, and a proud ego cannot handle failure. On one of the Bill Gaither tapes, Lulu sings a sweet Gospel song, *"Failure Is Not Final With the Father,"* but for the truly proud man, failure is accepted as final.

God's answer to failure is confession, which will bring forgiveness and a chance to start over, but such admission of wrongdoing is almost impossible for the proud person. Therefore, a guilt projection for such a one becomes a standard reaction to failure. Then the proud person crawls into a cocoon of pretense and loses touch with reality, often turning to drink or pills. What price pride!

Pride Separates Us From Our "Kingdom"

It is probable that all of us are building a "kingdom" of one sort or another. It may be a family, perhaps a business, or a career. We are extending our dominion beyond the borders of our own lives and exerting an influence in the lives of others.

Right now, here in America, we see many religious "kingdoms" under development and others that are on display. The popularity of independent churches with no ties to a denominational affiliation makes it easy to build a congregation around a personality, a doctrine, or a practice. Some good leaders with charisma and drive have built themselves religious monarchies that touch the lives of thousands of persons.

I never cease to marvel at the vision and faith of some of these men and women. The structures they build, the programs they sponsor, and the outreach into the community for godliness are models many seek to follow. Only eternity will reveal the good that has been accomplished by these leaders.

Unfortunately, people quickly make heroes of them. They are lauded, applauded, written up in the Christian press, and featured on Christian television talk shows. Only a truly humble person can keep this from producing great pride. Like Nebuchadnezzar, they sometimes begin to project that they built the kingdom or, at the least, accept the praise and adulation offered to them.

Pride's Separation

While writing this chapter, I received a phone call from a minister friend of mine who, through the years, has seen many moves of God come and go. He was invited to participate in a conference hosted by a well-known Christian television personality. He said he was deeply grieved with the high level of glorification and praise heaped upon this pastor. "It was like they were worshiping him," he said, "and the pastor seemed to revel in it." It is a shame that this pastor can't seem to learn from history. Jesus declared loudly, *"Worship the Lord your God and serve him only"* (Luke 4:8). It is proper to honor our leaders, but it is always wrong to worship them.

Daniel tells us of King Nebuchadnezzar, *"As the king was walking on the roof of the royal palace of Babylon, he said, 'Is not this the great Babylon I have built as the royal residence, by my mighty power and for the glory of my majesty?' "* (Daniel 4:29-30, NIV). This ultimate expression of pride brought the judgment of God upon the king, and he was separated from his kingdom. Pride still does the same today. God will share His glory with no one.

It is only fair to point out that Nebuchadnezzar had begun to fall years earlier as he let his personal pride immunize him from the revelation that God brought to him. While he would acknowledge the hand of God, he would not repent or submit himself to Jehovah.

Robert Clinton recently wrote, "Few leaders finish well. The ones that don't finish well predominantly lose in the middle game, not in the end game. In looking at leaders who don't finish well, I have identified six barriers that stop them. One is pride. There is a proper pride in recognizing who you are and operating out of what God's done for you, but there is also the danger of an inordinate pride, pridefulness."[2] It has well been said that a minister is already on his way down when he begins to believe his press releases.

Mr. Clinton is not the first to observe this. Many years ago, D.L. Moody wrote, "When a man thinks he has got a good deal of strength, and is self-confident, you may look for his downfall. It may be years before it comes to light, but it is already commenced."[3]

No matter how well the kingdom is established, if the founder or director allows pride to dominate his attitudes, he, and likely the kingdom, will fall. Haven't we seen more of this than we wanted to in the past few years? It was not an accident that God warned Israel, *"I will put an end to the arrogance of the haughty and will humble the pride of the ruthless"* (Isaiah 13:11, NIV). God is longsuffering, but He is neither blind nor hesitant to intervene in our inordinate pride. When we begin to play the role of God, we set ourselves up for serious chastisement. We can never get so high that God cannot bring us down. Sometimes we need to remind ourselves, *"Patience is better than pride"* (Ecclesiastes 7:8, NIV).

Pride Separates Us From God

It is bad enough to lose kingdoms through pride, whether they be individual or corporate, but to be separated from God by our pride is dangerous beyond comprehension. In His letter to the church in Laodicea, Jesus said, *"You say, 'I am rich; I have acquired wealth and do not need a thing.' But you do not realize that you are wretched, pitiful, poor, blind and naked. So, because you are lukewarm—neither hot nor cold—I am about to spit you out of my mouth"* (Revelation 3:17 and Revelation 3:16, NIV).

I have reversed the order of these two verses to point out that the cause of lukewarmness was their pride in possessions—their sense of independence from God. They were totally self-sufficient and really did not have an awareness of needing God. What a picture of the American Church! David could well have been a member of our society when he wrote: *"When I felt secure, I said, 'I will never be shaken.' O LORD, when you favored me, you made my mountain stand firm; but when you hid your face, I was dismayed"* (Psalm 30:6-7, NIV). This pride of self-sufficiency will separate us from God (not God from us). And we are never in greater danger than when God hides His face from us because of our pride.

How many churches that began on their knees crying out for God's divine intervention on their behalf became prosperous, influential, and independent of God? They function well without God. As a matter of fact, God seems to cramp their style when He does show up. Their pride may not cost them their premises or their prominence, but it will cost them the presence of God. And what is Christian activity without God's presence? Only religion. This is what so distressed Jesus when He walked among us.

Maybe we need to find a quiet place and let ourselves think. Is it more important for us to be seen or for Christ to be seen in us? Why do we so easily let ourselves believe what others are saying about us, when we know in our inner heart that without God we would be worthless sinners bound for Hell? It is only when Christ is lifted up that men are drawn to Him. If we are lifted up, people will be drawn to us, and what will we do with them? Let's return to being proud of Jesus and of what He has done and deliberately shun the spotlight that draws attention to the small part we have played in God's great scheme of redemption.

Endnotes:

1. James S. Hewett, *Illustrations Unlimited* (Wheaton, Il.: Tyndale House Publishers, Inc., 1988).
2. Robert Clinton in *Current Thought & Trends,* April 2001.
3. *Christian History*, No. 25, D.L. Moody.

Dear Jesus,

I have known too many times of separation from associates and from You because of my pride. Once again, I humble my heart to ask Your forgiveness. Please give me grace to think of myself according to the measure of grace You have given to me—and no higher. Don't let me begin to believe the accolades others offer to me. Help me to quickly pass them on to You, for all that is praiseworthy in my life is there because of Your presence. I would rather have Your presence than the praise of thousands of people.

Thank You for helping me once again.
Amen!

• • •

Questions

1. Robert Clinton says that pride is a barrier that keeps us from finishing well. Do you agree or disagree? Why? How could that happen in your life? What are you doing to finish well?

2. Think of an example or situation when pride has separated you from an associate, from yourself or from God.

Chapter 16

PRIDE'S PREJUDICE

In reply Jesus said: "A man was going down from Jerusalem to Jericho, when he fell into the hands of robbers. They stripped him of his clothes, beat him and went away, leaving him half dead. A priest happened to be going down the same road, and when he saw the man, he passed by on the other side. So too, a Levite, when he came to the place and saw him, passed by on the other side. But a Samaritan, as he traveled, came where the man was; and when he saw him, he took pity on him. He went to him and bandaged his wounds, pouring on oil and wine. Then he put the man on his own donkey, took him to an inn and took care of him. The next day he took out two silver coins and gave them to the innkeeper. 'Look after him,' he said, 'and when I return, I will reimburse you for any extra expense you may have.' Which of these three do you think was a neighbor to the man who fell into the hands of robbers?"   Luke 10:30-36, NIV

*O*h, how I wish I could say that pride was an Old Testament condition that was completely eradicated at the cross, but realistically, the New Testament abounds with illustrations of pride and exhortations against this insidious attitude. Jesus not only taught about pride's companions (see Chapter 19), but, Master Teacher that He was, He told stories that illustrated pride in action—usually without using the word *pride* in His story.

One such story is the parable of the Good Samaritan that Jesus told to a lawyer who was trying to *"tempt,"* or test, Jesus' knowledge of the Law. While we recognize that Jesus told this story basically to answer the lawyer's leading question, *"And who is my neighbor?"* (Luke 10:29, NIV), it carries an obvious subtheme of pride.

There are five unnamed characters in the story: a victim, a robber, a priest, a Levite, and a Samaritan. What great sermon material is available in this story! First we see a sinner who is robbed by Satan of everything valuable and almost destroyed in the process. He is ignored by religious authorities, but rescued and restored by the lowly Samaritan (who was despised by organized religion). What a picture of Jesus!

The setting of Christ's story is the steep and treacherous downhill road that spanned about twenty-one miles between Jerusalem and Jericho. Christ and His disciples had recently taken this route from Jericho. Since this wild road is proverbial for deeds of blood (even to this day), it is very likely that this parable was based on a fairly recent experience.

We remember that priests and Levites served in the Temple at Jerusalem by courses and that, when off duty, they went to one of the cities provided for the priesthood. Jericho was one of those cities, so it was a common sight to see priests and Levites on this route.

The Prejudicial Pride of the Priest

When the priest saw the victim, he moved to the other side of the road, probably to prevent being ceremonially contaminated. He had just come from a religious service—ministering sacrifices and sprinkling blood for the atonement of sin, but somehow he lacked compassion for the victims of that sin. He was proud of his office and his religious service, and that pride kept him from reaching out to those outside his religious sphere.

Jesus doesn't identify the nationality of the victim, but we presume he was an Israelite. This makes the attitude of the priest all the worse, for he was ignoring a fellow countryman who desperately needed help.

Before we condemn this man too severely, we need to remember that Christ *"hath made us kings and priests unto God and his Father"* Revelation 1:6. It is far too common for believer priests of today to be so holy that they are of no earthly good. They'll minister to anyone who comes to church, but they so fear contamination that they offer no help to the victims they pass every day in the real world. We sing of the great grace and love of God on Sunday, but our pride prevents us from displaying it in the places where sin is destroying lives.

We proudly boast of being an elder in the church or the chief vocalist in the choir, but on the Jericho road, we pull our robes around us and cross to the other side of the roadway. We are "off duty." We can't be bothered with the problems around us.

The tone of Jesus in this story is unmistakably condemnatory. It is interesting that this is the only record of Jesus censoring the priestly and Levitical orders. He seemed to respect their duties and dedication to service, even though He knew they were functioning out of religious duty rather than in relationship with God. Unlike the Pharisees and Sadducees who had added men's traditions to the written Law as God gave it, the priests and Levites continued to serve in the

Temple very much as God had commanded Moses to teach Aaron. Jesus knew that their time of service was about over and that the very Temple where they served would be destroyed in their lifetimes. He usually left them alone until He told this story.

Jesus couldn't tolerate the fact that the religious orders seemed so holy, and yet they were divorced from true love. And He still can't tolerate that! Although these men remained faithful to their religious duties, their pride in this service had permeated their lives. Their viewpoint in life had become a "holier-than-thou" attitude. One wonders how the Lord feels about the unmitigated pride so widely displayed by some of today's religious leaders.

In one of his great sermons, Charles Spurgeon said, "I think that it is one of the most difficult things in the world to love a proud man. You can love a man, even though he has a thousand faults, if he is not proud and boastful; but when he is very proud, human nature seems to start [pull] back from him."[1]

Is our personal concern for position or for people? Is pomp and ceremony more important to us than compassion and love? May God forgive us for confining our ministry to those within the walls of our particular church.

Adrian Rodgers recently observed, "We spend more time praying for the saved who are sick than for the unsaved who are lost ..., more time trying to keep the saints out of Heaven than the lost out of Hell."[2] Perhaps this is because most modern priests and Levites have almost no contact with people outside the church, and when they do make contact, it seems that those they encounter are in the condition of this victim in Christ's story—too far gone to be bothered with.

The Prejudicial Pride of the Levite

The tribe of Levi was chosen by God to assist the Aaronic priesthood. The Levites became the caretakers, service providers, and associate priests in the Tabernacle and, later, in the Temple. It would have been more in character for the Levite to minister to this poor victim than for the priest to do so. We will give him credit for at least taking time to look at the victim, but his assessment, for whatever reason, caused him to go on without helping the man.

With this Levite, it may have been a case of, "I'll look, but I won't touch," or "I'll talk to the man, but I won't get involved with him." Had there been such a service available, he probably would have called 911.

It's not too difficult to identify with this Levite. After all, if the priest wouldn't get involved, why should he? And why should we? What pride we display in suggesting that it really isn't our responsibility, especially if this victim does not go to our church or is not a member of our great denomination!

May I suggest that this victim reflects the many thousands of people alive today who have been deeply wounded and robbed by religion? Some have been stripped of all their savings and even their houses by unscrupulous religious leaders in their fund-raising schemes. "In the name of God," these people have been promised much, but given little.

When pastors change pulpits, they often do a major rearranging of staff and workers. It is natural for them to choose people with whom they are comfortable, and to bring key workers with them who have a proven track record of working well with the pastor. For all the good this offers, it does displace others who have held these positions in the church before the new pastor's arrival. Sometimes these former faithful workers are deeply wounded in the process of change.

It isn't fair to put the full weight of responsibility for wounded brothers and sisters on our pastors. Saints are often very brutal to other saints. All who have farm experience know that if a chicken gets pecked sufficiently to draw blood, the other chickens will attack it too, until the bird is killed. Similarly, if a brother or sister is even slightly wounded in the church, there are those who will continue to pick on him or her until the person is mortally wounded. Gossip, false stories, even the mere suggestion of wrongdoing, all have seriously wounded many Christians and have destroyed the reputations of others.

I would have had to keep a written record to know how many such persons have talked with me about this in conference settings. They meet me at the altar or sit with me at lunch and pour out their deep hurt. They still love God, but they have not yet recovered from the wounds their brethren have inflicted.

The wounded lie on the roadway of life outside of our churches in pain, disillusionment, and frustration. Since they no longer sit in the pews of our churches, they are bypassed by believer-priests. No one is pouring the oil and wine of the Holy Spirit on their wounds. Pastors and lay members (priests and Levites) cannot be bothered to bring them to the inn. They are just left to die by the wayside. We seem to be too proud to try to restore them to spiritual health, unless they come under the roof of our authority.

The Non-prejudicial Attitude of the Samaritan

To the shame of both the priest and the Levite, it was a Samaritan who showed compassion to this victim. He knew that if this victim was an Israelite, he had been taught that Samaritans were dogs and that to entertain one in the home was to lay up judgments for a house. The Samaritans were openly cursed in Jewish synagogues, and yet this one put his pride in his pocket and demonstrated unusual love and care. He refused to act in prejudicial pride. Instead, he seems to have been noble enough to help this wounded fellow traveler.

The town of Bandon, Oregon, where my father was then a pastor, burned to the ground in an out-of-control forest fire in 1936. Federal, state, and Christian organizations quickly offered relief and reconstruction to the distressed residents. Unfortunately, because my father was a pastor, none of these agencies would give him and his family any help. Their attitude was, "Let his denomination take care of him." The denomination in which Dad was serving the Lord had no program in place for helping in such disasters.

Dad put the meager possessions we had saved from the fire into the car he had preserved from burning by parking it on a bluff overlooking the ocean. We drove to a neighboring town where the owner of a bar and nightclub made room for us in the back of his facility and provided food for us. We stayed there for many days while Dad was searching for something better for his family. Eventually, an unsaved man offered us his garage, and we lived there for about six months. I have always had a soft spot in my heart for these modern "Samaritans" who had compassion on us when Christian believers were too self-occupied to help us.

Jesus put no names on these five characters, which makes it easy for us to identify with them. May God help us to leave our pride in the closet with our ecclesiastical robes when we step out of divine service. As we head for our homes after ministering before the Lord as either priests or Levites, let's remember that we are merely men or women with a call of God upon our lives.

Maybe it would help us to remember what Don Marquis said back in the early twentieth century: "Man thinks he amounts to a great deal, but to a flea or mosquito, a human being is merely something good to eat."[3] So why should we take ourselves so seriously?

Endnotes:

1. Charles Spurgeon, Electronic Database (Seattle: Biblesoft, 1997).
2. Adrian Rodgers, in *PrayerNet Newsletter*, October 2000.
3. James S. Hewett, *Illustrations Unlimited*, (Wheaton, Il.: Tyndale House Publishers, Inc., 1988), p.439.

O Lord,

Writing [in your case, reading] this chapter has been painful for me, for I identify with both the priest and the Levite. Please forgive me for having eyes only for those in the church. You died for the whole world, and You commissioned me to be Your agent in all of it. I confess that my pride has caused me to withdraw from and bypass needy persons when I was headed for a time of rest and recreation. Please forgive me and help me to humbly accept my mission to the wounded and suffering here on this earth. I need a new touch of Your compassion.

Thank You.
Amen!

• • •

Questions

1. Why is it difficult to love a proud person?

2. Who has been a Good Samaritan in your life? What did they do to merit that respect?

3. In what specific way is pride at the root of prejudice?

Chapter 17

PRIDE'S DESTRUCTIVENESS

A bishop then must be blameless, the husband of one wife, vigilant, sober, of good behaviour, given to hospitality, apt to teach; not given to wine, no striker, not greedy of filthy lucre; but patient, not a brawler, not covetous; one that ruleth well his own house, having his children in subjection with all gravity; (For if a man know not how to rule his own house, how shall he take care of the church of God?) not a novice, lest being lifted up with pride he fall into the condemnation of the devil. Moreover he must have a good report of them which are without; lest he fall into reproach and the snare of the devil. 1 Timothy 3:2-7

Take heed therefore unto yourselves, and to all the flock, over the which the Holy Ghost hath made you overseers, to feed the church of God, which he hath purchased with his own blood. For I know this, that after my departing shall grievous wolves enter in among you, not sparing the flock. Also of your own selves shall men arise, speaking perverse things, to draw away disciples after them. Therefore watch, and remember, that by the space of three years I ceased not to warn every one night and day with tears. Acts 20:28-31

*I*t is likely that more destruction has happened in the Church through pride than through overt demonic activity. Satan has no creative powers that enable him to replace demons that have been cast into the pit or elsewhere, so he is seriously understaffed. The world's population and the size of the Church continue to explode, but the devil has fewer personnel now than were available to him in the Garden of Eden. I have long said that if it wasn't for the help of Christians, Satan's work would never get done in the Church.

This enemy of Christ's Church knows our human nature better than we know it ourselves. He accomplishes much havoc and destruction in the Church merely by playing on some of the extremes of our humanity. One of his favorite ploys is to stir pride among the brothers and sisters. From that moment on, he can leave the destruction up to the believers and not have to be directly involved.

Overseers Are Essential

A group of people without leadership has the potential of becoming a mob. They may be swayed by emotion or by devotion, but they have neither goals nor direction. Following a move of God, often called a revival, it is common for groups of excited ones to gather together to share their experiences and joy. Unless a true leader comes forth among them, they are destined for a very short life as a segment of the Church. They will die from attrition or from atrophy.

When I was a boy, prepackaged chicken was not yet available. We had to butcher our own. Quite frequently, it fell to me to cut the head off the chicken we would eat for dinner. Once the head was severed, I would drop the chicken on the ground and watch it run in circles while wildly flapping its wings. It had great motion, but it wasn't going anywhere. It lacked the direction a head would have given it.

I have seen Christian groups that reminded me of one of those headless chickens. They expended energy, raised lots of dust, and had an abundance of motion, but they went nowhere and accomplished nothing. They needed leadership. They were severed from their head, Christ Jesus.

God, our Maker, knows how useless we are without leadership, so He provided for priests, pastors, elders, deacons, bishops, and other titled directors. They can be the difference between fruitfulness and frustration.

Overseers Must Be Mature

The apostle Paul was a church planter who had a passion to see what he had paid such a price to bring into existence continue to flourish in spiritual health and ministry. He never left a work he had established without appointing spiritual leaders to oversee that work.

As he faced a lengthy imprisonment and eventual martyrdom, Paul wrote instructions to Timothy and Titus about qualifications to look for in potential leaders. The list is quite extensive—reaching from moral issues to marital relationships. The emphasis in both the Timothy and Titus letters is on the importance of appointing mature persons to leadership. Paul specifically said, *"He must not be a recent convert, or he may become conceited and fall under the same judgment as the devil"* (1 Timothy 3:6, NIV). Paul felt that maturity, not personality, was the prerequisite for leadership.

I have a spiritual advisory relationship with a very special young man who is a senior divinity student at Vanguard University in Southern California. On his Christmas visit home, he came to my study to tell me that one of the professors had called him in for an evaluation talk. In effect, he said, "Roger [not his true name], we're pleased to have had you here at the University. You are a brilliant student who is consistently on the dean's list. You have great drive and good people skills. I'm convinced that you are going to make it big in the ministry for about ten or fifteen years; then you will fall and take down your church with you."

Shocked, Roger asked, "What do you mean? Why?"

"You are intellectually far more advanced than you are emotionally and morally mature," the professor said. "Unless you let us help you grow up into manhood and establish patterns of discipline and Christ-like behavior, you will fall as have so many before you."

Hurrah for Christian professors who are interested in producing mature leaders, not merely educated ones! And three cheers for the response of this young man! He is staying on at the school to earn his master's degree, while getting special tutoring in areas where he is underdeveloped. He wants to be a mature leader in the Body of Christ. I am convinced he will make it.

We are a nation obsessed with shortcuts. Almost tragically, we bring this fetish into the Church with us. I was shocked to receive an e-mail offer last week that promised a full ordination certificate for $29.95. It assures the reader that it is as valid as one offered by a recognized denomination. There must be a market for this or they would never advertise it. Men and women want leadership roles without preparation and training for those roles. We mistakenly believe that an anointing will always compensate for a lack of preparation. It can, but it rarely does.

Overseers Are Subject to Pride

Being in the limelight can be heady stuff, especially for a novice. Leadership has its privileges, as well as its responsibilities, and being in charge of others can give a leader an exaggerated sense of importance. All of this feeds the inherent pride that is abundant in each of us.

A pastor friend of mine saw great potential in a new convert and invited him into a discipleship relationship with himself. They met at least weekly as the pastor opened scriptural truths and leadership principles to this young man. After less than a year, this young man was nominated to be a deacon at an annual business meeting. To the horror of the pastor, this young convert was elected on the first ballot. He obviously had become quite popular in the church.

On their first meeting following the election, the young man asked the pastor, "Now that I'm a deacon in the church, don't I technically have authority over you?" It took only a few days for pride to manifest itself in this immature believer.

Pride in a church leader at any level becomes an instrument Satan uses against the church. How many churches have been split wide open by a proud associate who felt he could do a better job of leading the congregation! We saw this earlier in Miriam and Aaron, when they desired an equality of leadership with Moses.

In most American cities, we have a proliferation of very small churches that have been founded by proud persons who will not work with others, but lack the ability to do a decent job by themselves. They gather ambitious persons around themselves who are thrilled to be called elders or deacons. By keeping us divided by our pride, Satan succeeds in preventing us from succeeding in the mission of spreading the Gospel of Christ into all the world.

Proud Overseers Are Subject to Satan's Condemnation

Paul specifically stated that a leader in the local church should, *"Not [be] a novice, lest being lifted up with pride he fall into the condemnation of the devil" (1 Timothy 3:6).* I don't believe that this means the devil will condemn a proud leader, for why would the devil oppose one of his most useful tools? More likely, Paul warned that just as the devil was condemned for his pride and was separated from God while being deported from Heaven, so proud church leaders will find themselves separated from God and displaced from service in His Kingdom.

Pride's Destructiveness

Alfred Ells, a renowned Christian counselor in Phoenix, Arizona, says, "Pride is probably the major reason for a lack of favor with God and therefore lack of success in ministry. It is also the major root issue in failure."[1]

At the end of Paul's final missionary journey, as he was headed for Jerusalem, he stopped at Miletus and summoned the elders of the church from Ephesus. He gave them a tearful farewell speech, reminding them of how faithfully he had worked to produce that Ephesus church and how he had handpicked and trained these very elders. To their complete shock, Paul ended by telling them, *"For I know this, that after my departing shall grievous wolves enter in among you, not sparing the flock. Also of your own selves shall men arise, speaking perverse things, to draw away disciples after them. Therefore watch, and remember, that by the space of three years I ceased not to warn every one night and day with tears"* (Acts 20:29-31).

Church history attests that Paul's prophetic insight was correct. After Paul's martyrdom, pride divided these leaders, and they dissected the work with all the skill of a surgeon. Paul had lovingly invested years in establishing the Ephesus church, but proud elders took it apart in a short time.

The human heart is unchanged today. Pride still brings division, contention, and strife among Christian leaders. The glorious Church that Christ purchased with His own blood and for which godly men and women have paid such a price to bring into being often falls into the hands of proud leaders who are willing to destroy almost anything in order to have their own way.

You are probably aware of family-owned churches and deacon-run churches where the proud leadership crushes anything unpleasant to them. We know of other churches where the pastor views himself as the lord and master of the entire congregation and proudly rules with a heavy hand. Where is Jesus? Isn't it His Church?

What a high honor it is to be chosen to be a leader in the Church at any level! It makes us *"workers together with him"* (2 Corinthians 6:1). We are not workers *for* Him; we are workers *with* Him. We are not in charge; He is. The initiative is His. The ability is His. The responsibility is His. Of what, then, have we to be proud?

I believe that Paul's admonition to refuse to put a novice into leadership needs careful implementation in today's church, not only for the church's sake, but also to spare the immature believer from a strong temptation to develop pride that may destroy him. We have enough Christian casualties in our communities. Let's not kill another immature believer with our appointment or ballot to an office he or she is not ready to handle. Let's allow young believers to grow up before heaping leadership responsibility on them.

Endnote:

1. Alfred H. Ells, M.C. in *Counselor's Corner*, Vol. II, No. 257.

Dear Jesus,

I am one of the leaders in Your Church. Please surround me with persons and circumstances that will control my pride, rather than let my pride control me. Help me to grow in grace and in the knowledge of my Lord and Savior so I can share my maturity with young believers.

Thank You.
Amen!

• • •

Questions

1. What would you say to a new believer who has gifts of leadership and who wants to be released in ministry?

2. What was your experience of stepping into leadership for the first time? Were you vulnerable to pride?

Chapter 18

PRIDE'S PLEA FOR PROMINENCE

Then the mother of Zebedee's sons came to Jesus with her sons and, kneeling down, asked a favor of him. "What is it you want?" he asked.

She said, "Grant that one of these two sons of mine may sit at your right and the other at your left in your kingdom."

Matthew 20:20-21, NIV

Then James and John, the sons of Zebedee, came to him. "Teacher," they said, "we want you to do for us whatever we ask."

"What do you want me to do for you?" he asked.

They replied, "Let one of us sit at your right and the other at your left in your glory."

"You don't know what you are asking," Jesus said. "Can you drink the cup I drink or be baptized with the baptism I am baptized with?"

"We can," they answered.

Jesus said to them, "You will drink the cup I drink and be baptized with the baptism I am baptized with, but to sit at my right or left is not for me to grant. These places belong to those for whom they have been prepared."

When the ten heard about this, they became indignant with James and John.

Mark 10:35-41, NIV

When I hear a congregation proudly sing "Onward, Christian Soldiers," I realize that very few of the singers really mean what they are singing. Not too many Christians want to be a private, a mere soldier, in God's army. Most would like to be an officer, and some yearn to be a general, while the rest of us would at least like to have privileges at the officers' club.

We are willing to start following Jesus at any level, for each level available is a giant step above our life in sin, but most of us want fast promotions. Officer training school is out of the question. We want to go from being a private in boot camp to at least a lieutenant colonel as fast as possible. We may want to skip rank, but it isn't going to happen. God loves us too much to let us have positions of responsibility far beyond our maturity. It is not so much a matter of "paying your dues" or "working your way up the ranks" as it is a matter of learning to be faithful in a little, so we can eventually become faithful in much.

Pride That Entreats for Position

I think I see some of this at work in the passage we're examining. James and John made a prideful plea to Jesus to be positioned one on His right hand and the other on His left hand when He came into His glory. They wanted to be vice-president and secretary of state in the kingdom they expected Jesus to originate there in Jerusalem. That they were ambitious is obvious, and ambition is commendable, but they were allowing their ambition to create prideful levels of lust for position and for authority over the other disciples.

191

In some ways, these men were already Christ's right- and left-hand men. Together with Peter, they already formed the innermost circle of His associates. This triad, made up of Peter, James, and John, was present when Jesus raised Jairus' daughter from the dead. They witnessed the transfiguration of Christ, and they were summoned by Him for prayer support during His agony in Gethsemane. These men were active with the Lord at a level far greater than the other nine disciples were. They had been honored by Jesus to be with Him in very difficult situations, and they had been at His side in times of great glory. They were, obviously, very proud of this.

James and John possessed a fiery fanaticism in wanting to call down fire from Heaven on the Samaritan village refusing to receive Jesus and His disciples. This may have been why Jesus called these brothers "Boanerges," or "sons of thunder," in Mark 3:17. They were never passive in their service with Jesus. They were wholehearted, enthusiastic followers.

James and John—probably James's younger brother—were among the first disciples called into service by Jesus. They were also the two disciples whom Jesus commissioned to prepare the Passover meal for Him and the other disciples just before His crucifixion. It is obvious that they were trustworthy men with considerable insight into the heart of Jesus. In military parlance, they were aides to the General.

For all this greatness of service, however, these disciples had no titles. They were simply called by name. If they weren't on assignment for Jesus, they were on equal status with the other disciples. A competitive pride caused them to ask the Lord for a promotion in rank—for titles, for conferred authority.

Before we become unduly judgmental about what these men did, we need to take a long, hard look into our own proud hearts and into the hearts of many who are in divine service with us. There seems to be a pernicious and prideful lusting for titles of authority today. Disciples want to be called apostles, bishops, priests, or elders. These are Bible titles for leaders in Christ's Church and should not be taken lightly, but neither should we lust after them. Christ and the New Testament writers offer ministry to believers—even gifted ministry—but most Christians prefer to have a title, even if they have to award it to themselves.

In the years that I was a pastor, I saw how dangerous titles can become to believers. I found it difficult for persons to wear a title without succumbing to pride. Instead of serving, they paraded. Rather than minister in their giftings, they gloried in their positions. I see an amazing amount of this in the Body of Christ today.

In the last church I pastored, I publicly surrendered my title of pastor and chose to simply be called "Brother Judson." I then asked each titled person in the church to surrender his or her title as well. We simply made Jesus the Pastor, the Elder, the Healer, the Teacher, etc., and we took a position of serving with Him. This worked wonders in the lives of the individuals who gave up their appellations in the congregation, for it turned all eyes back onto Jesus.

James and John had an unusual closeness to Jesus, but closeness to the Lord should prompt worship, not yearnings for position. Christ draws us to Himself, not that we should replace Him or even develop an equality with Him, but that we may worship and adore Him. As we learn from the Tabernacle in the wilderness in the Old Testament, praise was an Outer Court ministry, but worship required being in the Holy Place. We can praise the Lord from a distance, but worship demands closeness to Him. This "inner circle" was the closest to Jesus of all the disciples. At the Last Supper, John took advantage of this closeness and laid his head on Christ's bosom, while Peter declared a loyalty to Christ even to death. As best they knew at the time, they were worshiping Jesus. It is difficult to be that close and not worship Him. His tender love flows out and elicits a return response of love, adoration, and devotion.

Pride That Expects Payback

What I have written is pretty much the standard interpretation of the request of these two young men as the gospel of Mark records the story. However, the Matthew account of this incident introduces the mother of James and John and shows her as the petitioner on behalf of her two sons. Why would these two "sons of thunder" need their mother to speak for them?

Perhaps a glance back at the history of that period will help clarify the picture. The woman in question is identified as *"the mother of Zebedee's sons"* (Matthew 20:20). Why? Zebedee was a fisherman who ran an extensive fishing business on the Sea of Galilee. He was based in Capernaum on the north shore of the sea. In addition to his sons, James and John, he employed hired servants to help him in his trade. Simon Peter and Andrew were among them.

The ministry of Jesus deeply affected the "Zebedee Fish Company," for the first disciples Jesus called to serve with Him were the owner's two sons, James and John. Two key employees—Andrew and Peter—quickly followed, quitting the fishing company to become followers of Jesus. Add to this the fact that, according to Mark 15:40-41, when Jesus was in the Galilee district, some women had *"followed him and cared for his needs."* The mother of James and John most likely was one of them.

The Bible account does not say if Zebedee ever became a believer, but he did not stand in the way of his sons, wife, and employees becoming Jesus' disciples. Not only did Zebedee temporarily lose his wife and permanently lose two sons and two dependable employees to the service of Jesus, it is very likely that when Jesus was in the Galilee district, He and His entire entourage stayed in Zebedee's home in Capernaum, enjoying the hospitality of the Zebedee Fish Company.

In the light of this great investment in Jesus and His ministry, it may not seem unreasonable for this mother to ask Jesus for special positions for her sons in His Kingdom. The substance of her petition probably was, "After all we've done for You, the least You could do for us is to give my sons a position of honor and authority with You. We have this coming." As a gambler would say, she was "cashing in her chips."

She does not stand alone in this attitude. We read, *"Peter answered him, 'We have left everything to follow you! What then will there be for us?'*" (Matthew 19:27, NIV). This must have characterized the attitude of all the disciples, for Jesus asked if they had a servant plowing in the field and he came in at the close of the day, would they have a meal ready for the servant, or would they direct the servant to prepare a meal for them? He concluded the story by saying, *"So likewise ye, when ye shall have done all those things which are commanded you, say, We are unprofitable servants: we have done that which was our duty to do"* (Luke 17:10). The concept of being "unprofitable" implies that we consume more than we produce. We are trainees—not actually earning our way in the company business. For all that we do, we are still a liability.

When I was diagnosed with cancer, I went straight to prayer, of course. I was shocked to hear myself pray, "Lord, after all I have done for You, why have You allowed this to happen to me?" I was foolishly projecting that I deserved better treatment than cancer. Sweetly and so very gently, the Holy Spirit spoke into my heart, "Judson, if you got what you really deserved, you would be headed for Hell right now." I quickly repented and began to praise the Lord for His excellent goodness to me.

In seeking to bring the Church back to a comfortable recognition of our authority in Christ and of His great provisions for us, teachers of our generation have caused some of us to feel we had a right to demand things from God. We have been taught that we can do a "trade-off" with Him—that if we give Him ten dollars, we can expect Him to give us a hundred dollars in return. We "invest" in another's ministry and expect a harvest in our own.

Some years ago, when I was serving on staff with Dr. Fuchsia Pickett in Plano, Texas, a returned missionary couple held a service for us. In talking with them, I realized that they needed to tour the United States in a GTM (get the money) ministry, and that they had no means of transportation. I had just purchased a new diesel-powered Nissan Maxima sedan that was my pride and joy. The Lord told me to give it to them, so I loaned it to them. Fifty thousand or more miles later, they returned the car with praise for its performance and an apology that deteriorating health would prevent them from returning to the field. As they handed me the keys, the Holy Spirit reminded me that God had told me to give them the car, not loan it to them. Asking them to wait a moment, I pulled the ownership certificate out of the file, went downstairs to a resident notary public, and signed the car over to them. This, of course, elicited hugs and many thanks.

I went for months having to use my wife's car or depend on others for transportation. I was waiting for God to replace my Maxima with something superior. After nearly a year had gone by, I asked God in prayer, "Where's the car You owe me?"

"What car?" He answered. "I don't owe you a car."

When I reminded Him of my obedience to His command to give my car to the missionaries, He said, "I didn't say invest your car. I said give it."

"But what will I do for a car?" I continued.

"If you feel you need a car, go out and buy one," He told me.

For nearly a year, I had felt God was obligated to me for obeying Him. How foolish, how prideful, and how unscriptural I was being!

Is it possible that Mr. and Mrs. Zebedee were "investing" in Jesus and expecting a return, rather than giving to Him out of hearts of love? Did they think they were earning frequent flyer miles that they were now turning in for a free ticket?

Like this mother and her two sons, we often plead our sonship with Jesus and demand the rewards of that sonship in the here and now. We try to convince God that we are invaluable to His work on earth and certainly deserve recognition and rewards. What inordinate pride! Whether we realize it or not, when we do this we reduce ourselves to the level of a hireling rather than live in the joy of being children of God and coheirs with Jesus Christ. We deserve nothing. We can earn nothing from God. Everything we obtain comes to us through His mercy and grace, not through an award system we have devised.

Will our hearts ever learn to be content just to be with Jesus? Will our pride forever insist that we be rewarded and honored for the limited service we offer to Him?

Dear Father,

How foolish I have been in trying to bargain with You. I am guilty of trying to cash in bonus points I really do not possess for favors with You I do not deserve. There are times when I really do feel that I deserve a position at Your right hand, especially when people are praising me for my ministry. Lord, I humble myself before You. Please forgive my pride that has produced superior feelings. Forgive me for giving because I expected to get even more in return. Let me live in the abundance of Your grace and expect nothing more than what You choose to give. Then, in love, help me to share this with others.

Thank You.
Amen!

• • •

Questions

1. Do you expect others to always use a title in addressing you? Why? How do titles help and/or hinder us in exercising authority or doing the work of the ministry?

2. Think of a time you expected God to do something for you in return for what you did for Him? Was pride a factor?

3. How do you identify with James and John and/or their mother?

Chapter 19

PRIDE'S COMPANIONS

And he said, That which cometh out of the man, that defileth the man. For from within, out of the heart of men, proceed evil thoughts, adulteries, fornications, murders, thefts, covetousness, wickedness, deceit, lasciviousness, an evil eye, blasphemy, PRIDE, foolishness: all these evil things come from within, and defile the man.

Mark 7:20-23 (emphasis added)

And then he added, "It is the thought-life that pollutes. For from within, out of men's hearts, come evil thoughts of lust, theft, murder, adultery, wanting what belongs to others, wickedness, deceit, lewdness, envy, slander, pride, and all other folly. All these vile things come from within; they are what pollute you and make you unfit for God."

Mark 7:20-23, TLB

*W*e have looked at the portraits of more than twenty persons who let pride negatively affect their behavior. The results of this pride were serious and often deadly. Pride out of control is a tyrant. Yet few proud persons are really aware of their pride, for pride wears so many different masks. Unfortunately, as we have seen, pride is the one disease that everyone around us seems to suffer from except ourselves. Usually we need a diagnostician among our associates to make us aware of its presence.

Jesus dealt with pride at every turn in the road. He had to rebuke it in His disciples, He exposed it in the rich young ruler, and He consistently exposed pride in the religious rulers just by His presence. He crafted His parables to expose pride in the human heart, and He lived in such humility that His life was a constant opposite of pride.

Amazingly, Jesus did all this without using the word *pride*, except in the scriptural passage we're now considering from Mark's gospel. Jesus was a masterful teacher. He taught without raising the defenses of His audience until the lesson had been heard in full. No wonder even His enemies had to testify, *"No one ever spoke the way this man does"* (John 7:46, NIV).

Jesus did not condemn, but He certainly brought conviction to His audience. He didn't pontificate on pride, but He presented a precise picture of it. His listeners consciously or subconsciously applied His teachings to their lives.

When Jesus finally did use the "P" word, He taught us two important things: (1) pride's companions, and (2) pride's source.

Pride's Companions

We learn much about a person by the company he keeps. People who drink generally associate with other drinkers. Cattlemen usually hang out with other cattlemen, and college professors associate with other educators. It is not often that lovers of Western music enjoy the opera. The cliché, "Birds of a feather flock together" in general fits all of us. It is not so much a matter of exclusivity as it is of commonality.

In Mark's account of Jesus' only use of the word *pride*, He listed thirteen vile things that contaminate our lives and pride is in the list— *"... evil thoughts, adulteries, fornications, murders, thefts, covetousness, wickedness, deceit, lasciviousness, an evil eye, blasphemy, PRIDE, foolishness"* (Mark 7:21-22, emphasis mine). We might not, but Jesus does. All of these actions are grounds for dismissal from ministry in most churches and even from holding church membership in many. But how long has it been since you heard of a person being defrocked from his or her ordination or losing membership in the church because of pride?

Imagine yourself standing in a police lineup with twelve individuals guilty of the above sins when your "only" sin was pride. I would expect a loud protest and a declaration that you were being unjustly condemned by association, but that is exactly what Jesus did when He shared this truth with His disciples. He condemned the proud by association, for sin is sin—no matter how small or camouflaged it is— and pride is often the root of much sin.

Because pride and foolishness are here listed last by Jesus, some preachers have declared that all the other dispositions flow out of pride. I think they could make a good case for this viewpoint. Pride does beget many other vices, and if pride goes to the cross, many of the other evils will go to the cross with it.

Because pride wears fancy robes and can change its appearance faster than an actor who plays all the parts in a drama can, we seldom see pride at work in our lives. However, Jesus sees it, our friends are mindful of it, and the indwelling Holy Spirit does His best to make us aware of it. Even when His conviction is strongly at work in our hearts, we find it difficult to admit, "I am the man."

Pride's Source

It is popular in some religious circles to declare that Satan is the source of our pride, but Jesus knew better. Satan was the originator of pride in the heavens, but once pride was introduced into the stream of humanity, it became an active part of our nature. Twice in this brief passage Jesus declares that pride is inherent IN US: *"For FROM WITHIN, out of the heart of men, proceed .... All these evil things come FROM WITHIN, and defile the man"* (Mark 7:21, 23). This is sobering. Jesus holds us personally responsible for all thirteen of these evils, and He says their origins are within a person, not outside of him. This includes pride.

God warned us through the pen of David: *"Whoever has haughty eyes and a proud heart, him will I not endure"* (Psalm 101:5, NIV). Pride is in the heart. David knew it, and if we are honest with ourselves, we know it too. We seem to have been born with proud hearts, and aside from a deliberate action on our part, that pride will grow more dominant in our lives as time goes by.

Jesus' list of evil attitudes and actions was basically repeated by the apostle Paul in Galatians 5:19-24, where he calls them *"works of the flesh"* (verse 19). He warns: *"They which do such things shall not inherit the kingdom of God"* (verse 21). Paul then puts these works in juxtaposition to the fruit of the Spirit, reminding us: *"Those who belong to Christ Jesus have crucified the sinful nature with its passions and desires"* (verse 24, NIV).

How wonderful it is that Jesus, Who knows us better than we will ever know ourselves, clearly stated that this pride is *in* us, not *outside* of us. It is not a great demonic force coming against us like a tornado from which we are unlikely to escape. Rather, it is a living force within us that is subject to crucifixion by identification with Christ. We can contain it, conquer it, or crucify it. Paul says that death on the cross is the preferred treatment.

Pride's Antithesis

We often learn best by seeing a truth in contrast to something else. Jesus loved to teach in this way. In this matter of pride, He did not merely give us contrasting words, as Paul did in comparing the works of the flesh to the fruit of the Spirit. Jesus went beyond words and let His life be a continuing contradiction to pride.

God loves to reveal the false by merely presenting the truth. Just as the presence of genuine currency for comparison will reveal the flaws in counterfeit money, Jesus was such a meek man and lived such a life of humility that pride was consistently exposed in others by way of contrast. He did this in two ways—by His nature and by His actions.

Jesus was humble by nature. Actually, He was (and still is) God's ultimate example of humility. Philippians 2:5-11 is often called the *kenosis* ("self-emptying") of Christ. It lists seven downward steps Christ took in coming to earth as Jesus, and then it lists seven upward steps He took in being restored to resplendent glory in Heaven alongside the Father. Under the inspiration of the Holy Spirit, Paul wrote: *"Who, being in very nature God, did not consider equality with God something to be grasped, but made himself nothing, taking the very nature of a servant, being made in human likeness. And being found in appearance as a man, he humbled himself and became obedient to death—even death on a cross!"* (Philippians 2:6-8, NIV). This incarnation is evidence of Jesus' heavenly humility. He didn't become humble after He got to earth; He was humble in the heavenly realms.

Jesus' entire life on earth, from His birth in a manger to His death on a cross, was evidence of His humility. He, who was the God-man on earth, chose to take the form of a servant in demonstrative humility. He testified: *"Even as the Son of man came not to be ministered unto, but to minister, and to give his life a ransom for many"*

(Matthew 20:28, see also Mark 10:45). What a contrast to the proud religious rulers of His day!

Jesus' very atonement was an act of humility: *"He humbled himself and became obedient unto death"* (Philippians 2:8). It was not His sin that sent Him to the cross—it was *our* sin. It is difficult to make a case that God was responsible to redeem fallen man, but Jesus, in humility, took our place, paid our debt for sin, and redeemed us back to fellowship with God.

Even Christ's ascension and exaltation to the throne, where He is now crowned with glory, was (and is) an act of humility. We may never know throughout all eternity what the crucifixion cost Jesus. As far as we can understand, the atonement was complete when Jesus cried from the cross, *"It is finished"* (John 19:30), but for our sakes, Jesus humbled Himself and took His glorified human body back to Heaven, where He has accepted its limitations. It is true that He is exalted and glorified, but He now lives in His humility in the perpetual limitations of a body.

Jesus, being humble by nature, was equally humble in His actions. Look at the men He called to be His associates—fishermen, a tax collector, farmers; they were very common men. Jesus ministered to the lowly people. We read: *"The common people heard him gladly"* (Mark 12:37).

In a day when women were little more than household slaves, Jesus showed tenderness, graciousness, and honest consideration to women. Since His coming to earth, wherever the Gospel has been preached, the status of womanhood has been elevated. Jesus did not make second-class citizens of the women He met. He humbly embraced them as fellow citizens of God's Kingdom.

The entire ministry of Jesus is a lesson in humility. He not only cleansed the lepers; He was willing to touch them. He could speak healing to people without touching them, but He usually laid His hands compassionately on the sick as He healed them. He was compassionate to the sick and suffering and showed concern for the hunger of the multitudes who had spent the day listening to Him teach. Rather than take an offering from them, He miraculously fed them with multiplied loaves and fishes.

Perhaps Christ's ultimate act of humility shown to the disciples was girding Himself with a towel and washing the feet of each one of the them. This was too much for Peter, who protested—unsuccessfully. When Jesus had finished, He told them, *"For I have given you an example, that ye should do as I have done to you. Verily, verily, I say unto you, The servant is not greater than his lord; neither he that is sent greater than he that sent him"* (John 13:15-16). Jesus wanted this demonstrated humility to become a part of their lives. He displayed more humility to His disciples in this one act than He could have taught in a dozen sermons.

The power of Jesus' words about pride, as recorded by Mark, is greatly amplified by the example of His life, which was absolutely free from sinful pride. No one could speak about pride with more authority than Jesus could, and when He spoke, He left little doubt about how dangerous, damaging, destructive, and divisive pride is. He let us see pride's companions and then contrasted this with His life and ministry of perfect humility. I believe that just as Jesus said to the lawyer, to whom He had told the parable of the Good Samaritan, He wants to tell us today, *"Go and do likewise"* (Luke 10:37, NIV).

If we hear only the words of Jesus speaking about pride's companions, we will likely cringe in self-condemnation, but if we will look at the life of the One who spoke those words, we will dare to believe that there is a way out of our sinful pride.

Dear Jesus,

I don't think that I have ever seen pride as hideous as You picture it in the one time You name it. Please help me. I don't want to be associated with those evil sins of the flesh. Forgive me for holding on to pride when You have been asking me to release it to Your cross.

Jesus, will You implant a measure of Your glorious humility in my life? I want my relationships with others to flow out of true humility, not a false humility. Let my lips and my life be in agreement in this matter of humility so that I may have a closer relationship with You.

Thank You.
Amen!

• • •

Questions

1. Who is the most humble person you know? List his or her qualities of humility.

2. What are some ways you could exercise humility to express the opposite of the spirit of pride? For example:

   • Write an anonymous note of encouragement to someone who needs it.
   • Pray for someone each day this week, but don't tell him or her and see what happens.
   • Give a gift to someone or make a contribution to an organization without letting anyone know.
   • Do a task for someone at home, at work, in your neighborhood or church, but don't tell anyone you did it.

Part III

THE SOLUTION TO THE PROBLEM

Chapter 20

GOD'S PRESCRIPTION FOR REMOVING PRIDE

Having said this, he [Jesus] spit on the ground, made some mud with the saliva, and put it on the man's eyes. "Go," he told him, "wash in the Pool of Siloam" (this word means Sent). So the man went and washed, and came home seeing.

His neighbors and those who had formerly seen him begging asked, "Isn't this the same man who used to sit and beg?" Some claimed that he was. Others said, "No, he only looks like him." But he himself insisted, "I am the man."

"How then were your eyes opened?" they demanded.

He replied, "The man they call Jesus made some mud and put it on my eyes. He told me to go to Siloam and wash. So I went and washed, and then I could see."

"Where is this man?" they asked him.

"I don't know," he said.

They brought to the Pharisees the man who had been blind. Now the day on which Jesus had made the mud and opened the man's eyes was a Sabbath. Therefore the Pharisees also asked him how he had received his sight. "He put mud on my eyes," the man replied, "and I washed, and now I see."

John 9:6-15, NIV

*7*n the beginning of this book, I suggested that pride was basically an "I" trouble. I spelled the word *p-r-I-d-e*. Proud persons have a distorted view that magnifies themselves as greater than others and, sometimes, greater than God.

It is interesting to me that every type of miracle Jesus performed had also been done by someone in the Old Testament, with but one exception. Until Jesus came, no one had ever opened the eyes of the blind. Yet the gospel writers record more instances of Jesus healing blindness than of any other type of miracle He performed.

Please forgive me if I sound extreme in saying that, for illustrative purposes, I see a correlationship between this and pride. Is it possible that after our redemption our greatest need is to have our spiritual eyes opened? Perhaps we are like puppies whose eyes must open after birth.

Isn't pride a blindness? Perhaps it is tunnel vision for some, but for most of us, it is a total inability to see beyond ourselves. We have become like a television set that can receive only the "me" channel.

In healing the blindness of the man in our Scripture lesson, Jesus did not merely speak the word, as He had done when healing blind Bartimaeus. He chose to use both means and participation. He molded a piece of clay and placed it on the man's empty eye sockets; then He told the blind man to actively participate in the miracle.

"Go wash in the pool of Siloam," Jesus had said. This is repeated three times in the story, as the blind man was quizzed by spectators and then by the Pharisees. Now the formerly blind man, he was very much aware of his active participation in receiving his sight. He had searched for the pool, gotten into it, and washed his eyes. That was

not an easy task for a blind man. Why did Jesus do it this way? We don't know, but it certainly gives us a powerful example of our need to participate in the riddance of our pride.

In removing our pride-induced blindness, we must become an active participant. Pride is not taken away by merely having a "great one" lay hands on us and pray. If we seriously want to be rid of pride-blindness, it will likely require a searching and a bathing on our part. Jesus will match our actions with His miracle of restoring us to 20/20 spiritual vision, but removing pride is a "God and I" operation.

Preventing Pride

We've learned that wearing dark glasses on a bright sunny day, especially when around sand or snow, will prevent eye damage. Prevention is better than a cure—both naturally and spiritually. Anything we can do to prevent the entrance of pride into our spirits will save us the long search for our Pool of Siloam.

Aside from having a problem with our inherent pride, we often have a problem with projected pride. People are often gracious enough to share their opinions of us to our face, and sometimes those opinions are very flattering. If received and believed, they will breed pride in our hearts.

Thomas Merton said, "The humble man receives praise the way a clean window takes the light of the sun. The truer and more intense the light is, the less you see of the glass."[1]

As I mentioned in Chapter 2, early in my traveling ministry, I would deny what people said as they expressed their appreciation for my ministry. I would ask them to not praise me, but to praise God. One day God rebuked me for treating His people unkindly. He told me to accept every compliment with grace and thanksgiving, and to hold it in my hand like a delicate flower until the end of the day. Before going to sleep at night, I was to gather all of these flowers into a bouquet and present it to the Lord in praise. I have made this a habit for nearly twenty years. It works. I can smell the flowers during the day, but I deliver them to God at night. I realize all day long that the praise belongs to God and will be given to Him in the evening. I have no basis for pride. I'm just holding God's flowers.

We can do ourselves a service by keeping short accounts with pride. Deal with it the very day it manifests itself, if not the very instant it begins to stir you. Pride, like all other vices, can be best destroyed while it is still a small seed that has not yet sprouted. It doesn't take a pick and shovel to remove a stray seed from a flower bed, but these tools may be needed to dig out the roots of a mature plant.

Purging Pride

Unfortunately, we don't always handle pride quickly, and it rapidly takes root and begins to blossom and bear fruit. It appears to belong in the garden of our hearts, but, in reality, it is nothing more than a nasty weed.

Let me share a quote from Andrew Murray. He writes, "In all heaven and earth, pride and self-exaltation are the gate and the curse of hell."[2] It is painful to realize that pride is the root of all evil in our lives, but it is, and removing it will clean up many other evils in our hearts.

Pruning the plant of pride may beautify it and keep it from standing out in the garden too prominently, but its roots will crowd out the roots of humility, and that which we cut off will rapidly grow back. This plant must be removed from our hearts—roots and all—or we will never enjoy the glorious presence of God in our lives.

How do we remove pride? That question must be answered by each individual, but five basic principles can be shared. We need to recognize it, reject it, repent of it, remove it, and replace it.

Recognize It

The first step for pride removal is, obviously, to recognize it in our lives. We will never deal with pride until we identify it. The purpose of this book was to make pride recognizable, but it is possible to read the book and only recognize pride in the Bible characters we have mentioned, but not in ourselves. We quickly and easily see pride in others, but we cannot deal with pride in others. We can only deal with it in ourselves, and we must.

God has given us two major sources for identifying personal pride: a source outside ourselves—friends (and even enemies), and a source within ourselves—the Holy Spirit. Listen to what your spouse or your friends tell you about your pride. If you react in anger, it is proof that pride is present. When praying, don't do all the talking. Give the Holy Spirit a chance to speak to you. He'll lovingly point out your areas of pride.

Just as the placement of mirrors in an automobile may leave us a blind spot for traffic, we all have blind spots in our character that are easily seen by others, but unrecognized by ourselves. Trust the passengers to do some of the seeing for you. It may well prevent a tragic accident. It takes a big person to recognize and admit personal pride, but there will be no deliverance from it until that happens. Like the blind man, we need help in getting our problem to Jesus.

Reject It

If we can recognize pride in our lives, we need to reject it, and the sooner the better, for it is an insidious source of evil. If we don't repel pride quickly, we will soon have other vices with which to deal. Close the door to pride, and don't answer the phone when it calls. Reject it!

Reject your need to be right. It's only pride. Reject anger, irritability, and impatience as a mere appendix to your pride. Reject the need to be seen as the "great one" in always being called by your titles or degrees. Frankly, who cares—except you?

As we have seen in the preceding chapters, pride is a great actor and is very capable of presenting itself as someone very different. Get so you can recognize it and reject your relationship with it. Ignore pride's costume and mask. Check its footprints. Pride leaves distinctive tracks.

Be on guard when around proud persons. Pride is an infectious disease transmitted by mouth. A proud person will brag you into a vocal contest that will soon cause you to try to top him. His pride soon becomes yours.

Repent of It

If we have determined to reject pride as it is revealed, we need to take the third step and repent of it. Pride is more than a mere attitude; it is a sin, for it exalts ourselves above our God. It demands its own way, as opposed to God's way. Yes, pride is a sin, and it seems to enter our lives like a pregnant queen bee. It soon reproduces itself again and again...until it has an entire hive of pride working for it.

How much better off the human race would be if Adam and Eve had repented of their pride before it blossomed into rebellious disobedience. Similarly, our families will be better off, and the family of God will be blessed, if we quickly bring our pride to the cross of Christ. Remember, pride dies more readily when it is young.

I think I can guarantee that we will not repent of our pride until we see it as the hideous menace God's Word declares it to be. Much as Internet pornography seems so innocent until the victim finds himself completely ensnared by it—often to the destruction of his marriage and ministry—pride seems so innocent until it has rendered us totally incapable of functioning in the truth.

Yes, pride is nothing short of sin, and God's answer to sin in the lives of believers is clear: *"If we confess our sins, he is faithful and just to forgive us our sins, and to cleanse us from all unrighteousness"* (1 John 1:9). Our confession of sin and our repentance from sin brings into action the work of Christ's redemptive sacrifice at Calvary. God forgives, Christ's blood cleanses, and the Holy Spirit places us back into fellowship with the Triune God.

Pride that had become a barrier between us and God's presence will be torn down, dissolved, cleansed, and inactivated by the application of the blood when we repent, but not until we repent. It is *our* pride, and God won't violate our free moral agency by removing it from us without our permission. Like the blind man, we must be active in this process of forgiveness and restoration by confessing and repenting.

May God grant to us the spirit of the publican who cried so very simply, *"God, have mercy on me, a sinner"* (Luke 18:13, NIV). No one needs mercy more than a proud person. He is set on a course of self-destruction, and he will systematically alienate his friends.

This thing called "pride" is too big for us to handle alone. It will out-think, outsmart and outmaneuver us every time. When rebuked, it will take on a false humility and promise to behave itself. When attacked, it will go into hiding. If we try to pull it out like a weed, it will break off at the surface, but the roots will remain alive and ready to grow a fresh plant. We need outside help to eradicate pride from our hearts, and that help is Jesus. His divine help is available by dialing 473-7368 (I-REPENT) on your prayer phone.

Remove It

A fourth step I suggest in handling personal pride is to remove it from your life. "But," you might say, "I thought that was what Jesus did when I confessed it as a sin." Well, not quite. Let me explain. I live in the desert in Phoenix, Arizona, and my yard is covered in crushed granite. In theory, this should preclude any need for maintenance. In reality, the hardness of soil, the lack of moisture, and the heat of the desert sun, don't deter the weeds from growing through the gravel. I can quite easily kill them with a weed spray, but the weeds, now withered and dried, remain. It is necessary to completely pull them out to have a well-manicured yard. Identifying with the cross of Christ will remove the life from our pride; it will poison it, but its skeletal structures will remain. Dig them up. Pull them out. Get rid of every remembrance of them.

Paul reminds us: *"Ye have put off the old man with his deeds"* (Colossians 3:9). The imagery is the removal of a coat in preparation for putting on a different garment. The "deeds" Paul speaks of are enumerated in the context—eleven serious sins of the flesh, most of which spring from pride. Paul says to strip them from your life like a dirty shirt. God has something better for you to wear, and that something better is what we are to *"put on."* Paul continued *"[You] have put on the new man, which is renewed in knowledge after the image of him that created him"* (Colossians 3:10).

Replace It

We don't have to live in pride. God has made us new creatures in Christ Jesus. Paul reminded the saints in Galatia: *"As many of you as have been baptized into Christ have put on Christ"* (Galatians 3:27). He further told the saints in Corinth: *"We have the mind of Christ"* (1 Corinthians 2:16). We've already seen that Jesus was God's perfect model of humility. There was no pride in Him. If we put off our pride, we can put on Christ and enjoy the humility of His mind, rather than struggle with the pride of our minds. What freedom! What liberty! What a divine exchange!

Ah, but there is more. Read on to the next and final chapter.

Endnotes:

1. Thomas Merton (1915-1968), *Bible Illustrator for Windows*, Ver. 3.0 (Fremont, Ca.: Parsons Technology, Inc., 1990-1998).
2. Andrew Murray, *Humility*, (Pittsburgh: Whitaker House Publishers, 1982).

Dear Lord,
I am so tired of this nasty pride that has afflicted me all my life. It has blinded me to real values and caused me to go by feeling instead of reality. I want to be free from it. I ask for a cleansing of my soul and spirit, and I also ask for the help of the Holy Spirit in removing every vestige of pride from me. I don't even want to be reminded of these terrible weeds. Please open my eyes, first of all, to the lingering pride in my life that needs to go to the Pool of Siloam, and secondly, to the glorious grace of humility that You are eager to share with me.

Thank You.
Amen!

• • •

Questions

1. Do you have difficulty receiving praise? Why?

2. How is false humility the same as pride?

3. Which of the suggestions I provide to handle pride are helpful for you?

Chapter 21

PRIDE'S PROPER REPLACEMENT

To some who were confident of their own righteousness and looked down on everybody else, Jesus told this parable: "Two men went up to the temple to pray, one a Pharisee and the other a tax collector. The Pharisee stood up and prayed about himself: 'God, I thank you that I am not like other men— robbers, evildoers, adulterers—or even like this tax collector. I fast twice a week and give a tenth of all I get.'

"But the tax collector stood at a distance. He would not even look up to heaven, but beat his breast and said, 'God, have mercy on me, a sinner.' I tell you that this man, rather than the other, went home justified before God. For everyone who exalts himself will be humbled, and he who humbles himself will be exalted."   Luke 18:9-14, NIV

And whosoever shall exalt himself shall be abased; and he that shall humble himself shall be exalted." Matthew 23:12

A man's pride shall bring him low: but honour shall uphold the humble in spirit.   Proverbs 29:23

*M*uch as a doctor's written prescription frequently contains a single word for the brand name of the medicine, so God's prescription for pride in our lives contains but one word: *Humility*. It is a simple, fundamental, readily available remedy, but it is quite bitter to take. It is neither buffered nor sugarcoated, but it comes in various dosages. Sometimes the pill is so large it nearly chokes the proud person, but if he or she can get it down, it will cure the patient of pride.

We considered the removal of pride from our lives in the preceding chapter. We know that all nature abhors a vacuum, but do we know that our spirit also deplores a vacuum? Jesus tells a story in Matthew 12:43-45 about a man who was cleansed from a demonic spirit but did not make room for the Holy Spirit as a replacement. Jesus said that the displaced spirit, discovering its former residence cleaned but empty, would return with seven other spirits worse than himself. I think it very likely that if we merely remove pride, but do not replace it with a positive force, pride will return with reinforcements so that our second state will be worse than our original condition.

Humility Displaces Pride

The proud fisherman who boasted to Jesus at the Last Supper, *"If I should die with thee, I will not deny thee in any wise"* (Mark 14:31) wrote, *"Be clothed with humility: for God resisteth the proud, and giveth grace to the humble"* (1 Peter 5:5). Peter's failure at the arrest and trial of Jesus exposed his empty pride, and Christ's appearance to him after the resurrection seems to have served to replace that pride with humility. In the first division of the book of Acts, we see a very different Peter than we see in the gospels. When humility replaced his proud boasting, God used him mightily in the early Church.

Dwight L. Moody (1837-1899), the great evangelist of a past generation, said: "A man can counterfeit love, he can counterfeit faith, he can counterfeit hope and all the other graces, but it is very difficult to counterfeit humility."[1] Counterfeit humility, or false humility, as we commonly call it, is nothing more than pride wearing a humble-looking garment. It is distasteful to everyone who sees it, and it is an abomination to God. It is pretense, it is hypocrisy, it is deceitful, and therefore it is patently sinful. False pride is not a displacement for pride; it is a display of pride in costume.

Humility is more easily demonstrated than defined. The entire life of Jesus was a demonstration of humility. Someone has said, "Humility is recognizing that God and others are responsible for the achievements in my life."[2] Jesus consistently said that His works were merely the works He saw His Father do, His words were the words He heard His Father speak, and His will was consistently submitted to the Father's will. That's humility in action!

Andrew Murray (1828-1917) wrote a short book titled *Humility,* in which he sought to define this wonderful attitude of life. He wrote: "Humility is perfect quietness of heart. It is to have no trouble. It is never to be fretted or irritated or sore or disappointed. It is to expect nothing, to wonder at nothing that is done to me. It is to be at rest when nobody praises me and when I am blamed or despised. It is to go in and shut the door and kneel to my Father in secret, and be at peace as in the deep sea of calmness when all around and above is trouble."[3] For some reason, I don't see an excess of this type of humility in the modern Church, but then, humility cannot take root and flourish until pride is removed from the life.

When Humility Returns, Restoration Begins

When Nebuchadnezzar's pride brought God's judgment upon him, he lost everything—including his mind. Somewhere in this seven-year season, he humbled his heart and God began a process of restoration. His counselors and lords returned to him, the kingdom was restored to him, and he blessed the Most High God. He humbly recognized that all he possessed came from the hand and divine will of God.

It is equally so in our own lives. Pride will destroy, but humility will restore. This is what Peter had in mind when he wrote, *"Humble yourselves, therefore, under God's mighty hand, that he may lift you up in due time"* (1 Peter 5:6, NIV). James had learned the same secret, for he wrote, *"Humble yourselves before the Lord, and he will lift you up"* (James 4:10, NIV).

Through the years, I have repeatedly watched pride entice a Christian leader into sin that brought him or her to ruin. Somewhere in this great humiliation, pride was replaced with humility, and I've watched God restore such persons to ministry again—sometimes to an even greater ministry than before. Please know that it is not sin that humbles us, but grace. In the pride of our activity for God and His kingdom, we may lose sight of His wonderful grace until we find ourselves in a place of desperation where we either receive divine grace or perish. It is at this point that humility makes possible the process of restoration.

Around 400 A.D., Saint Augustine of Hippo wrote, "It was pride that changed angels into devils; it is humility that makes men as angels."[4] Recognizing the desperate need for humility, and knowing that it comes from a warm relationship with the grace of God, many have taught the value of daily sinning so we could regularly partake of God's fresh grace. It was to this error that Paul wrote, *"What shall we say, then? Shall we go on sinning so that grace may increase? By no means! We died to sin; how can we live in it any longer?"* (Romans 6:1-2, NIV).

We need not fall deeper and deeper into sin to rise to greater and greater humility. True humility is not looking down on yourself, but looking up to Christ. The closer we get to God, the lower we will be in our own estimation. Phillips Brooks (1835-1893) put it this way: "The way to be humble is not to stoop until you are smaller than yourself, but to stand to your real height against some higher nature that will show you how small your greatness is."[5]

True Humility Affects God's Attitude Towards Us

Holman's Bible Dictionary tells us, "Ahab, the seventh king of Israel's Northern Kingdom, married a foreigner, Jezebel, and incited God's anger more than any of Israel's previous kings."[6] The list of the combined sins of these two individuals fills many chapters in the Old Testament. God pronounced a severe judgment upon both Ahab and Jezebel, but almost surprisingly we read, *"Then the word of the LORD came to Elijah the Tishbite: 'Have you noticed how Ahab has humbled himself before me? Because he has humbled himself, I will not bring this disaster in his day, but I will bring it on his house in the days of his son'"* (1 Kings 21:28-29, NIV).

His change from pride to humility spared this wicked king from God's judgment. Interestingly enough, Jezebel, who was proud even while being assassinated, was not spared. Obviously, she did not humble her heart before God. I seriously doubt if any of us have the means or the power to sin at the level Ahab sinned, but he changed God's attitude toward him by humbling his heart. It will work for us, too.

I have chosen as the Scripture lesson for this chapter Luke's account of the short parable in which Jesus compares the prayers of the Pharisee and of the publican, or "tax collector," as he is called in the New International Version. This passage certainly paints a striking portrait—contrasting the religiously proud person with the humble man. The Pharisee bragged to God about himself, while the publican pleaded for God's mercy. Jesus said of this Publican, *"I tell you that this man, rather than the other, went home justified before God. For everyone who exalts himself will be humbled, and he who humbles himself will be exalted"* (Luke 18:14, NIV).

This word *justified* means "not guilty" in God's sight. How vividly this illustrates what Jesus said, *"And whosoever shall exalt himself shall be abased; and he that shall humble himself shall be exalted"*

(Matthew 23:12). Also, with a small child sitting on His lap, Jesus said, *"Whosoever therefore shall humble himself as this little child, the same is greatest in the kingdom of heaven"* (Matthew 18:4).

Looking to Andrew Murray again, we hear him say, "Humility, the place of entire dependence on God, is, from the very nature of things, the first duty and the highest virtue of man. It is the root of every virtue."[7] No wonder it so radically affects God's attitude towards us.

Sincere Humility Changes Our Relationship with God

Andrew Murray also said, "Humility is not so much a grace or virtue along with others; it is the root of all, because it alone assumes the right attitude before God and allows Him as God to do all."[8] So humility not only changes God's attitude toward us; it also changes our attitude toward God, and this is essential. The proud see God as their servant, but the humble see Him as their Lord. He is not our equal; He is far superior to anything we can find in humanity. He is the Creator; we're only the created. He is in charge of our lives; we are not. The key to our salvation is not that we love God, but that He loves us and gave Himself for us.

Pride excludes us from God's presence, while humility becomes a point of entrance into God's presence. The prophet Isaiah wrote (in the voice of God): *"For thus saith the high and lofty One that inhabiteth eternity, whose name is Holy; I dwell in the high and holy place, with him also that is of a contrite and humble spirit, to revive the spirit of the humble, and to revive the heart of the contrite ones"* (Isaiah 57:15). God, being supreme, has the right to choose who will dwell with Him. He declares that He opens His door to the humble-spirited individual. Our pride will always separate us from God, but humility draws us into His presence.

Perhaps some who are praying for revival and a renewed sense of the presence of the Lord should take a look at the level of pride in their hearts. If they would handle their pride, they would find themselves enjoying the realized presence of the Lord, for He "dwells" with the humble.

True humility seems to have a low place in the priorities of American churches, perhaps because we have pride on such a large scale, but God maintains humility on His list of priorities. Andrew Murray wrote, "God places humility on the highest throne of the universe. Such is God's justice!"[9] Those who so aspire to go higher in God need to learn to go deeper in humility. Oswald Chambers insisted, "The great characteristic of a saint is humility."[10]

Yes, humility is God's prescription to prevent a reoccurrence of pride once we have successfully removed it from our lives, but it seems to me that it is like an allergy prescription. We must take a pill every morning, and another pill at night during the height of the season. But it is worth it, for, as Anne Austin reminds us, "Pride is the cold mountain peak, sterile and bleak; humility is the quiet valley, fertile and abounding in life, and peace lives there."[11]

Endnotes:

1. *Bible Illustrator for Windows*, Ver. 3.0, (Fremont, Ca.: Parsons Technology, Inc., 1990-1998).
2. Ibid
3. Andrew Murray, *Humility*, (Pittsburgh: Whitaker House Publishers, 1982).
4. *Bible Illustrator for Windows*.
5. Ibid
6. *Holman's Bible Dictionary for Windows* (Fremont, Ca.: Parsons Technology, Inc., 1990-1998).
7. Andrew Murray, *Humility*.
8. Andrew Murray, *Humility*.
9. Andrew Murray, *Humility*.
10. Andrew Murray, *Humility*.
11. *Bible Illustrator for Windows*.

Dear God,

In reading this book, I have seen more about pride than I ever wanted to know. What I have seen cuts me to the quick, for at one time or another, I think all these forms of pride have had a lengthy residence in me. Lord, I have denounced them as You revealed them to me. I believe that by identifying with Your finished work at Calvary, I have been cleansed from the guilt of these prides.
Now, dear God, help me to learn to put on humility. Give me the servant spirit Jesus ministered in. Help me to esteem others better than I esteem myself. Keep giving me Your prescription as many times a day as I need it. I don't ever want to forget that I must be humble or I'll stumble.

Thank You.
Amen!

• • •

Questions

1. How has this book helped you recognize pride and desire humility?

2. List examples of humility in Jesus' life.

3. How does humility connect you to God's grace?

Other McDougal Books

JUDSON CORNWALL

IT'S GOD'S WAR

A BIBLICAL VIEW OF
SPIRITUAL WARFARE

ISBN 1-884369-86-3 $9.99

by Judson Cornwall

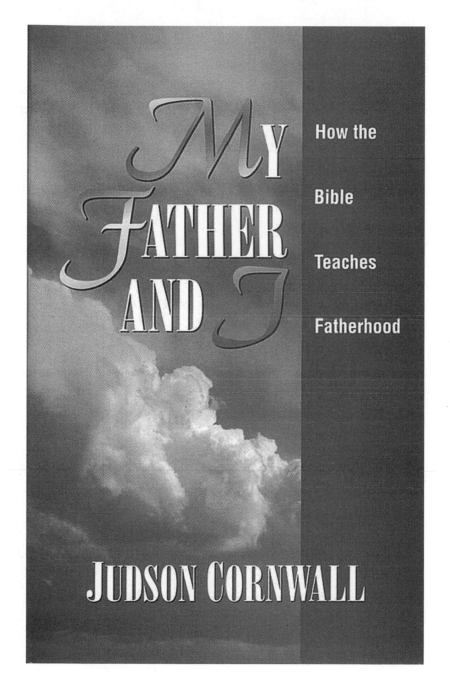

My FATHER AND I

How the Bible Teaches Fatherhood

JUDSON CORNWALL

ISBN 1-884369-78-2

$10.99